PRODUCT DEVELOPMENT
AN INTEGRATED APPROACH

David Inwood and Jean Hammond

KOGAN
PAGE

First published in 1993

Kogan Page Limited
120 Pentonville Road
London N1 9JN

© David Inwood and Jean Hammond, 1993

British Library Cataloguing in Publication Data
A CIP record for this book is available from the British Library.

ISBN 0 7494 1004 3

Typeset by BookEns Ltd, Baldock, Herts.
Printed and bound in Great Britain by Biddles Ltd, Guildford and Kings Lynn

Contents

Introduction—Perspectives on Product Development

All companies have 'products' (either tangible or services) and in a rapidly changing world, all companies should be concerned with the process of new product development (NPD). Many industries have become very good at effective NPD and balancing the many factors that affect it, often because of their exposure to rapidly changing consumer markets. Others exist in more stable environments where product development has been more evolutionary and sedate. Companies with technological products, however, seem to suffer from high levels of failure—either in the market, or with developments that never reach the launch point. Why is this?

One of the reasons is that in many markets, the space within which new products can be successful is becoming increasingly squeezed—due to the operation of three main forces (figure 1.1):

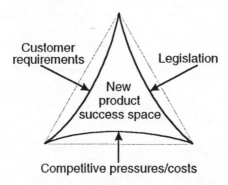

Figure 1.1 Market pressures on new products

Where such situations exist (and this is a growing number), a holistic approach to new product development (NPD) is required;

the traditional design or engineering led methods run too much risk of missing their target in 'new product success space'.

This introduction attempts to illuminate the breadth of the new product development process. It highlights the interdependence of a large number of factors that are all too often considered separately —if at all! No one can claim that NPD is simple, but a rational framework *can* be offered to guide companies concerned with improving the success of their developments. The framework is based on three different views of the process:

1. The company's perspective
2. The customer's perspective
3. The team's perspective.

It highlights the main techniques which will contribute towards successful NPD:

Total product management: developing all aspects of a product, not just its looks and how it is made;

Simultaneous engineering: the rapid and parallel development of marketing, industrial design, engineering and production;

Risk management: deliberate planned activity to allow the phased reduction of risk from any source;

Marketing: 'the management activity which seeks to anticipate and fulfil customer requirements profitably';

Team building: the activities that lead to good team work and enable the rest to happen.

This multi-disciplinary approach is referred to as 'Integrated Product Development' (IPD).

CONTEXT

The main tool of product development is, in its most general sense, 'project management'. Although our approach to this subject is new and broader than most, it is actually applicable to many other situations unrelated to new product development.

Although aimed at developers of products with a technical content, the approach that has been evolved is equally applicable to most projects (although some aspects of the techniques of goal definition will obviously differ). In fact, *any* project will benefit from an approach that explicitly asks:

- Why are we doing this? (the company's perspective)

- What will satisfy the recipient? (the customer's perspective)

- How do we go about it? (the team's perspective)

Insufficient attention to any one of these questions is likely to lead to failure.

THE COMPANY'S PERSPECTIVE

This book is written primarily for development team members and leaders. What is said about the company's perspective on projects is also aimed at this readership. What can team members and leaders learn from the top tier of the company that can guide them in their actions? What questions should they be asking of company directors to make sure they are properly informed?

People involved in projects should take every step they can to understand their project from the company perspective: this should put the project in the context of the company's mission and strategic direction. It helps people understand where their project fits in to the larger framework of product and market planning. It should also help people to weigh up the importance of their projects against others that the company is supporting. This in turn should help to explain some of the difficult resourcing decisions that have to be made at senior levels.

Strategic direction

The 'top down' approach to direction finding can provide a clear set of questions from those concerned with company purpose down to the nitty-gritty activities that keep noses to the grindstone. It is useful to know in theory what questions should be answered even though we all know just how different it all is in practice. If you as a project team member ask the right questions you may even find that there is an extremely useful mission statement lurking in the wings. It is also important to have some understanding of the actual techniques used to translate this strategic direction into product development programmes. The British Standard, BS7000 gives some guidance on how this can be done, and this is expanded in chapter 1.

Ultimately the point of carrying out new product development at all is to implement the company's strategic plans. There should therefore be a direct mapping between the company's objectives and the objectives of projects. If this can be achieved, it also opens up new ways for linking project success to company success and the possibility of rewarding teams in a manner that is fair to them (because it is linked to project goals), and fair to the company (because it is directly linked to company success).

The philosophy of Total Quality brings the company's perspective as close as possible to the customer's perspective by defining quality as conformance to customer requirements. It demands that strategy development is market led, ie not led wholly by the company's technology and other capabilities. What meaningful effect should this philosophy have on project team members? This topic is developed in chapter 5.

Do you understand what your company's generic marketing strategy is? Does it consider itself a market leader? Has it established a niche market? Whatever the strategy, can you see what impact it might have on your project and on NPD in general in the company?

Integrating development

According to a conference organised by the UK's Department for Trade and Industry (DTI) in December 1991, 'being fast enough into the market, with the right product, is worth more to the prosperity of most businesses than probably any other single management or manufacturing action'. Later sections of this book begin to shed some light on what makes 'the right product', but what are the company issues that affect the speed of reaching the market? The most influential of these is what has become known as 'simultaneous engineering'.

Simultaneous engineering

It is obvious that no product can be launched until all aspects of it have been developed. Until recently (outside Japan at least) the most common way to do this was for an idea to be turned into a design by the (technical) product development team, the design to be turned into a product by production engineering, the means of manufacturing this (tooling, fixtures, training and so on) to be created by the production team and finally for marketing to launch and sell the product. The norm has been for these processes to take place sequentially in what is often referred to as 'over the wall development', with very little continuity between the phases.

The Japanese motor industry has pioneered and proved the

worth of a new approach that creates integrated project teams representing all these phases and develops the various strands in parallel. Thus outline market research will be done simultaneously with exploring the technical possibilities and, at the same time, production will be investigating, planning etc. These techniques have been proven to reduce total development lead times from concept to launch by at least 50 per cent. But this depends absolutely on putting enough effort into the early phases.

There is a popular misconception that this term means that the normal phases of development should be run in parallel. This would actually destroy many of the gains possible from the techniques. For example, unless concepts and specifications are adequately defined, it would be suicidal to try to run technical, production and marketing development simultaneously. One of the big lessons learnt from companies that have successfully used simultaneous engineering is that attention to and investment in these early phases is extremely valuable—as long as these are integrated across *all* the disciplines involved in NPD. This does not mean that phased NPD should be so rigid that the needs of individual projects can't be catered for. One project might need a rapid prototype during specification, but if this is not allowed by an over-rigid structure, unacceptable risks might have to be taken.

Accepting that product development is a much broader activity than technical design is important because it opens up some concepts and areas of influence new to the traditional 'design & development team' and the integrated approach described in this book then becomes a real proposition.

Organising to encourage ideas—the raw material for NPD

All new products start life as 'just an idea'. These can legitimately come from *any* source, internal or external, and companies must work hard to eliminate the worst aspects of ownership often associated with this. Departments and people should be regarded more as conduits for ideas than owners of them. NIH syndrome (Not Invented Here) is rife in technical companies and is a real barrier to effective, rapid and successful development. This is all the more important when you realise that ideas need other ideas to feed on— rarely does 'a good idea' come into existence on its own; more frequently it is stimulated by examining other ideas, or only makes sense in conjunction with something else. Organising to allow for free communication and ready receptivity to new concepts is vital. The way people are grouped and teams structured have a real influence on the quality of ideas at this early stage.

Types of 'new' product

From the customer's point of view, a product is more than just the physical thing you develop—it includes service, packaging and certain intangible elements. Indeed, it can be argued that in every market the 'total product' is different. This introduces the concept of the 'product-market', where changes in either the product or its market are seen as developments of the whole, with proper consideration needing to be given to all aspects.

What does this mean? Launching an existing product into a new market should become a 'product-market' development activity, with the need to ask whether the match between product function and customer value is good enough, and what adaptations might need to be made to the 'total product', with the larger team being involved in the process. It also encompasses the fact that products and markets have life cycles, and customers behave differently at different stages in these cycles (eg the innovative purchaser has different expectations to the 'late majority' who buy during product maturity). It can be seen that the word 'new' in NPD can mean a whole spectrum of things from simple adaptation (of the core product or its packaging etc.) through major re-design to extend life and ultimately replacement with a completely new product.

This introduces the topic of risk. Any change is associated with some risk—the larger the change, or the more aspects that are changed at once, the bigger the risk will be. Entering a new market with an existing product always involves risk, as does developing a new product for an existing market. Much larger risks are involved, however, if both changes are attempted at once—ie during diversification. In the same way, incremental change to an existing product

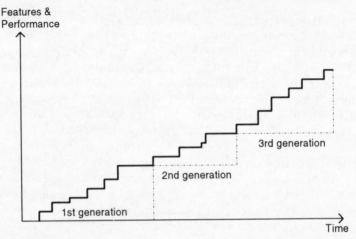

Figure 1.2 Incremental product development

is less risky than developing a completely new product. However for some reason it is seen by technical development teams as being less glamorous and there always seems to be resistance to this incremental development route.

This step-wise approach (Figure 1.2) is faster and cheaper as well as being safer than the more revolutionary developments. This is because small projects are inherently quicker and more cost effective than larger ones. The larger teams required by larger projects require disproportionately more management and are often less efficient in working and communicating. Every product development entails risk, the greater the scale of the development the greater the risk. If it is possible to develop incrementally, do so.

Setting priorities

If we accept that product development is essential to any company's long term health, how much should be spent on it and how should individual projects be prioritised? In the light of the material in this section, the latter question is now much easier to answer: project priorities must flow from company objectives, and projects must be structured so that their returns can be assessed at intervals and priorities adjusted accordingly (ie phased projects with dispassionate reviews).

To answer the question of overall scale we need to look at the relationship between various factors and long term profitability. Reinertson* has looked at the sensitivity of profit over five years to various forms of development failure (Figure 1.3). This shows that it can be very expensive to economise on development costs at the expense of shipping late or not achieving the desired product quality. Although the study was specifically on the market for printers, the results will apply to most markets subject to rapid change.

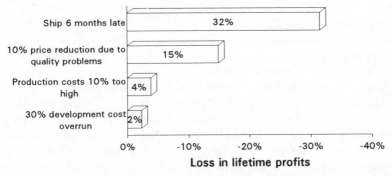

Figure 1.3 Effects of project failure

*Reinertson, D G (1983) *Whodunnit? The search for new product killers*, Electronic Business, July.

Another study* has shown the strong relationship between development spend and company profitability (figure 1.4). Other research
has shown that on a macro-economic scale this is reinforced by a
strong link between percentage of GDP spend on development and
rate of growth of GDP (UK being lowest at 2 per cent spent on R&D
with 1.5 per cent growth, Japan highest at 10 per cent spent on R&D
with 5 per cent growth).

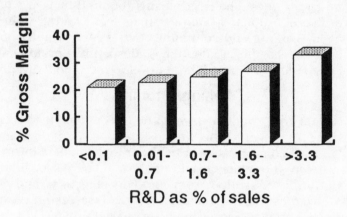

Figure 1.4 R&D improves gross margin

All of these factors would indicate that the importance of R&D
activity is largely underestimated by UK manufacturing industry.

Allocating resources

Possibly the last piece in the jigsaw of product development is the
way companies organise themselves to provide the resources
needed to carry out their chosen developments. There are a large
number of organisational models to choose from, and the choice
should be heavily influenced by the company's strategic plans. If
the company moves away from 'over the wall' techniques, then the
traditional departmental or functional organisational structures
will certainly have to be reassessed. In some cases a project centred
organisation may be the best solution, but more often one or other
of the possible implementations of an organisational matrix will
prove best. This is discussed in more detail in Chapter 6.

Whatever structure is adopted, conflicting demands of different
projects and responsibilities outside the project structure will
almost certainly arise. Solving these is a key aspect of project management and senior management. Understanding the organisation,
its goals and priorities is an essential part of this.

---

*Collier, Mong and Conlin (1984) *How Effective is Technological Innovation?*,
Research Management, Sept/Oct.

THE CUSTOMER'S PERSPECTIVE

Before embarking on any project it is vital to understa
are trying to satisfy. Unless you can identify the custom.
cannot adequately define what the project must achieve to ᴜ
cessful. It is also important to realise that there will usually be s
eral different customers for any one project. In the case of a product
development project these will include:

- The final users of the product;

- The distributors and retailers (your company's direct customers);

- Others in your company (and in that of the suppliers) who will
  implement your designs.

Having identified who your customers are, you now have to work
out how to achieve 'customer satisfaction'. This rather vague term
can be subdivided into four topics—'The four Cs':

- Customer value;

- Cost;

- Communication;

- Convenience.

— Assignment 2

We will deal with each of these in turn.

Customer value

Ultimately, as a result of your project, you are hoping to achieve a
fair exchange of value. You expect your customer to reward your
company (or you) with money (or kudos) in return for producing
something the customer values. Clearly, for this exchange to take
place with the largest possible reward, you must understand
exactly what will produce this customer value. There will often be
several elements to this. One of these will almost always be some
tangible product which in itself performs certain functions, and this
will normally need to be packaged or presented in a suitable way.
The product may also need installation, training and support before
it can be of value to the customer. Very often a product will be
bought for reasons other than the obvious physical thing itself (eg
for the image it conveys of the user or owner), so this should also be
regarded as part of the product development.

   In the case of some products, the tangible result of your efforts
will not produce anything of use to the end user without being augmented by other products, often from other companies. Examining

the utility the *total* product is intended to supply to the user will help identify third parties you should involve in the development process. For example, the average personal computer consists of hardware (often coming from several different manufacturers), environment software such as BIOS; operating system and desktop (more suppliers); and finally the application software that carries out the functions that the user wants (yet more suppliers). Only when all of this comes together does the user have a product that delivers any value or utility.

All of these elements will be important in determining the ultimate value the customer places upon the 'product' you deliver. Understanding all these component parts and processes gives you the opportunity to maximise the reward. This package, consisting of the tangible product (the physical item itself, including packaging) plus the intangible product (image, guarantees, support, disposal etc.), is often referred to as the 'total product'.

Cost

Companies tend to think in terms of the *price* of their products, whereas the customer is concerned with the total *cost* of purchase and ownership. At its simplest, this is just the other side of the customer value equation—ie, what the customer will pay for the total package that is 'the product'. Normally, however, the subject is more complex than simply determining the end-user price. A policy towards charging for all elements of the product as described above (installation, training, support etc.) will have to be determined. In some cases the 'total cost in life' must be thought through. This will entail examining the use of and cost of disposables (such as energy) and costs associated with the ultimate replacement and disposal of the product at the end of its useful life.

In many markets the company does not have any direct control over what is normally the largest element in the cost equation—the actual cost to the end-user. How this relates to the ex-works price (which the company *can* control) can be complex. The relationship will depend on channel length and structure (ie how many intermediaries there are between the company and the end-user and how much they mark-up the product), discounts for volume and prompt payment, who pays for marketing costs, and many other factors. As a product development team you will rarely have control over many of these factors. Yet they will have important effects, not only on the success of the development programme in the market, but also on the way in which some products should be developed. For example, you may see an opportunity for a better product and one which is slightly cheaper to manufacture than a similar product from a competitor. However, if that competitor is selling direct to end-users (eg via mail order) whereas your company normally sells via distributors and then retailers, you will have a real problem in competing with their customer cost of purchase. In a similar vein, you may be competing against a company that subcontracts its manufacturing (and hence has to pay transportation and supplier mark-up), in which case you may have a fundamental advantage by the time this difference is reflected and magnified in the *customer* cost. To offset these factors you will have to compete in other areas of producing customer satisfaction.

Communication

Often overlooked in technological new product development is the whole subject of how the customers are going to discover and understand the benefits of what you are creating. The old adage of 'build a better mousetrap and the world will beat a path to your door' is well proven to be wrong.

The elements that are commonly overlooked are:

1. making sure you can communicate the benefits of your product *in a way that is meaningful to the customer*; and
2. the availability and nature of a cost effective channel of communication to your market.

During the development process it is vital to re-appraise periodically how the features being developed can be communicated effectively and to test this. An understanding of communications theory is valuable here; it is not enough to know that you can create what you believe to be a good *message*; you also have to know that it is appropriate to the *medium* of communication to be used, and that the recipient will interpret the message in the way intended, without serious interference from competitive messages. For example, during the development of a new type of consumer product you must be aware that advertising is often only capable of delivering very simple messages (the 'single minded proposition', to use advertising jargon). If you are developing a completely new feature or function, can you be sure that the target customers will understand the benefit they might get from it? Given the ease (or otherwise) of communicating this, will they perceive the value of it as being enough to justify the expense of developing it?

Convenience

The easiest way of approaching convenience is to ask: 'How does the ultimate customer physically obtain the product?'. This leads to an examination of how the product is distributed from your company, through intermediaries to the eventual retailer/reseller. The storage and transportation questions raised should provide useful guidance to some aspects of the design of the deliverable and its packaging.

Summary

As a result of adopting this approach you should know everything you need to know about the ultimate deliverables from your development project. The most important lesson to learn is that the nature, content and cost of the project deliverable *must* be examined from the customer's point of view. Once you know what this is, you can then start to define what you have to do to achieve it. This is often an iterative process, and a better understanding of what can be done may alter the project's objectives. If this happens, go back over the thinking about the customer's viewpoint: in some cases a compromise solution will not produce enough 'customer value' to be worth pursuing.

THE TEAM'S PERSPECTIVE

Project scope and structure

It is very rare that product development will take place in a single set of activities, starting with defining the project's objectives and finishing with shipments to customers. This may be because the scale of the development is too large, perhaps involving several co-operating suppliers (as in PC development, outlined earlier). Even when only one company is involved, it is often necessary to divide the overall development programme up into more manageable sections (see Chapters 3 and 6).

When a product development is sub-divided into separate projects, the vision of the larger goal must be maintained. This may involve the introduction of tiered management responsibility, but experience shows that ultimate responsibility for success must rest with one person, not a committee.

Whatever the reason for sub-dividing a development, it is vital that you understand the scope of the project you are involved in, and the structure of the greater programme that delivers the total product. The scope is defined by the precise deliverables from your project. This could be a definition of the product concept, or a complete set of production documentation. Whatever your output will be, it is vital that it is properly and unambiguously defined. The structure of the larger project also needs clear definition. Obviously the sum of the parts must be made to equal the whole, ie the product development must be sub-divided so that every conceivable part of 'the total product' is being developed by someone. Less obvious, but just as important, is the need to structure the development into phases.

The British Standard BS7000 ('Guide to managing product design') begins to address these issues and provides a useful reference to a typical structure for the development process. There are, however, several important issues not covered, some of which are addressed in this book.

Risk

Product development is never a certain thing, with fixed and knowable goals at the start. The essentially fluid and adaptive nature of the process must be acknowledged by the adoption of a phased approach. This allows the right decisions to be made at the right time. Each decision will involve the commitment of company resources (whether money or people) and the level of this commitment must be commensurate with the risk involved. The overall process must be seen as the phased reduction of risk and the growth of certainty.

At the outset the level of risk—both technical and marketing—will normally be very high. As development proceeds, not only will risk reduce (although not in a linear fashion), but knowledge will increase. This knowledge will often cause surprise—the technology turns out to have unexpected capabilities, or new research sheds a different light on the market requirements. Product development must be adaptive to these surprises, and be capable of making the necessary decisions. Sometimes these decisions can be hard—such as the axing of a favourite idea. Harder still, however, can be the implementation of the changes in direction required by compromising what is technically possible with what will produce value in the market. Nevertheless, these decisions must be made, and made at the right time to avoid wasted resources and enthusiasm. This should not be regarded as a licence to be unthinkingly reactive to change. All such changes should force a re-examination of the impact on the larger project and, if necessary, cause earlier phases to be revisited.

Risk is, however, a much broader subject than this, and one very often ignored during the planning process. The adoption of the phased approach goes a long way towards addressing this, but a structured way of identifying and planning for risks is also essential. An approach to this subject is suggested later in Chapter 3.

Team membership

To achieve serious time and quality gains from this approach, the development team *must* include all relevant disciplines from the earliest possible stage (see the earlier section on Simultaneous Engineering). The expectation in these cross-functional project teams should be for change and easy entry and exit. These teams are at best not static; membership is constantly changing. Attitudes of the core or longer term team members should be to welcome and actively encourage participation by more peripheral members. This is not easy to achieve, and is one of the areas discussed in Chapter 4.

Team membership should include customers and suppliers as well as people from different functions within the company.

Team building

It will be clear from the previous section that building a project team is not a one-off process. In a working environment of constant change, pressure, responsiveness to customer demands and multiple links within and outside the company, there are two main objectives in improving team building:

1. To make sure that each working team understands at any time how it fits in to the overall picture of what the company is aiming to achieve.
2. To make sure that the best possible combined effort comes out of each team by taking a systematic approach to getting it up and running. How to work through this in practice is described in Chapter 4.

Planning and control

Fortunately the subject of project planning and control is well understood to be a key ingredient for success. As a result there is a plethora of management tools and techniques available as an aid to project managers. However, it is still vital to make intelligent and informed decisions on which tools to use. There are no universally correct answers, although there are at least some universally correct principles that can be applied.

One failing that is very common in this area is to view a project as a self-contained, logic bound entity. There is an increasing trend in product development towards projects which in reality are limited more by resources shared between projects and other company activities than by 'logic'. However, most management systems and most available software packages cannot effectively cope with this.

CONCLUSION

It must be clear from what has been said so far that successful new product development depends on a wide variety of skills and entails attention to a large number of different areas of the business. However, if success is the goal, then integration must be the key to achieving it. Product development must not be seen as a separate activity, but one that i) is integrated into the strategic thinking of the company, ii) focuses on existing or latent market needs, iii) requires skilled management and careful organisation. It also demands a new breed of people to contribute to or control the process —people who can manage the interfaces between all the disciplines required for successful product development.

THE STRUCTURE OF THIS BOOK

As the title suggests, this book is intended to provide detailed practical guidance on how companies can develop better products and bring them to market faster. To achieve this, everyone involved in product development must understand the issues and techniques involved. The book should therefore prove invaluable to corporate strategists, product managers, project managers and team members alike, whether they are from a technical, marketing or managerial background.

The essential principles, as have been outlined in this introduction, are that companies must first understand what will produce success (in *all* its dimensions), and then create a team capable of delivering this.

Chapter 1 looks at how to gain an understanding of the company's and the customers' perspectives of the development goal— how the product fits in with corporate strategy and what are the market's requirements of it. Chapter 2 deals with how this understanding can be converted into a precise product specification, and how this can be optimised to produce the best combination of customer value and reward for the company.

Arguably the whole book addresses the main risks involved in new product development. Chapter 3, however, provides a framework within which these risks can be approached, and shows how the main risk control techniques are applied to NPD.

It is *people* who carry out the process of NPD. Chapter 4 covers how a cohesive team can be built from the different disciplines required. Chapter 5 shows how these different people can work together as an effective team. Chapter 6 deals with how to structure and organise the make-up of these teams at different phases of the product development process, and shows how teams themselves develop to become more effective.

The relationship between the goal of the development and the team that delivers it must be contained in a model—the project plan, so that everyone involved or affected knows what to expect and when. This, and the specific control actions appropriate to NPD, are covered in chapter 7. Chapter 8 summarises the key elements of integrated product development.

1

The Goal—
Companies and Markets

Before describing the systematic process of new product definition in detail, it is useful to review exactly why developing the right product is essential for every company. The thinking applies equally well to any form of product which a company controls (eg by owning the intellectual property), including service products. It is aimed therefore at all companies who have control of the product element of the marketing mix. The process is not intended to apply to companies that produce what could be described as commodity products, ie where the product is not in itself distinguished from competitors, but who compete by superior control of the other elements of the marketing mix (ie price, promotion and place).

WHAT ARE PRODUCTS FOR?

A simple view of the primary function of any company is *the utilisation of resources to generate profits*, where profit is the surplus of revenues over the costs of generating them. For this to happen, the company must create something (either tangible products or services) which its customers value more highly than the cost of creating, supplying and supporting them. Anything that achieves this trick is, in these terms, a product.

This highlights the key function of a company's products—they exist to generate value. For this to happen two key elements must exist. First, there must be someone to buy the product—customers. Secondly, the products must fulfil some need; they must provide some utility that customers value. The question is, who are these customers and which of their many needs is the company trying to fulfil? This will obviously depend on the nature of the company and what it is trying to achieve.

There is a saying that 'if you don't know where you are going, any road will get you there'. Experience in business would seem to indicate the exact opposite, ie companies without a strong sense of direction don't achieve much compared with those who have a well developed mission and an agreed set of objectives. This should be obvious—senior management within any company is entrusted with a limited set of resources (including money, equipment and people). It is their task to satisfy the needs of those who provide these resources (ie shareholders, employees and the community) by utilising them effectively.

Many other organisations will be competing to achieve similar aims, so the main tasks a company faces is to distinguish how their own particular experience, resources and skills can be used to provide some *differential advantage* and set the priorities that enable these to be realised. To produce a differential advantage the company must be able to distinguish itself from competitors in ways that lead to profit. This will simply not occur unless a specific train of actions takes place. This is often called 'top down direction finding', but in reality it is not a linear process but an iterative one which takes into account not only the requirements of the stakeholders (the providers of the resources), but also the environment in which the company operates (the market) and its unique attributes (strengths and weaknesses). Those companies that focus their energies on areas where they have (or can create) some competitive advantage will thus be able to improve their long term profitability. Conversely, companies that do *not* focus their development efforts will soon end up with a diverse portfolio of products that is inefficient to support, market and develop further.

It is not the object of this book to provide any detailed discussion of these techniques. What is vital however, is for senior management and product developers alike to understand this key point: **Products are the primary means by which companies achieve their objectives.** If you accept that there are two fundamental competitive strategies available to companies—cost leadership and differentiation—and that cost leadership is really only available to the largest supplier in any industry due to economies of scale, then it is clear that creating and developing new products is the major competitive tool required to achieve effective differentiation. This means that not only must those responsible for managing product development understand what the company has to achieve through its products, but senior management must also understand the needs of product development when they set the company goals. This is an important point that should force a new clarity of thinking upon corporate planners. Their output must provide a *usable* framework within which product development takes place; this book attempts to provide such an approach.

WHY DEVELOP NEW PRODUCTS?

Having established the role of products within the company, we need to be clear about the requirement to develop *new* products. Referring back to points made earlier, there are two main pressures. The first comes from customers. In the developed world at least, virtually every group of customers (industrial or individual) are themselves developing. They are becoming better educated, exposed to more and better communications and hence they are becoming more discerning, with higher expectations. The very act of consuming or using products changes the consumer.

The second pressure comes from every other organisation that is trying to exchange its products for those customers' money. Some of these will be competitors, in the traditional sense of providing products of equivalent or substitute function. However *any* organisation selling *anything* to your customers has the same aim— to maximise their income from that source. They are thus competing with you. These companies are also aware of the increasing expectations of their own consumers, and if threatened by the introduction of a new product into the market, their reaction is often to introduce an improved version of it, or to reduce their prices to tip the cost/benefit balance in their favour.

The world is getting ever more sophisticated, and those companies who are succeeding best are becoming increasingly *customer focused*: they are going to greater lengths to make sure they understand what their customers value, and provide it more effectively than their competitors. Part of this greater effectiveness comes from faster introduction. A company that can develop and launch a product to meet a changing or emerging need can soonest reap great rewards (see the Reinertson study mentioned in the Introduction).

The three core elements for success from more effective NPD are therefore:

Assignment 2

1. being customer focused;
2. producing differential advantage through products; and
3. getting them into the market rapidly.

Whilst many companies are striving for these things, achieving them is difficult, particularly the last one. Succeeding in all three should be the goal, but given the difficulties, being very fast with something good enough can actually produce competitive advantage on its own.

These pressures should not be seen as a threat to product development, but as a great opportunity. Those companies who adopt the techniques discussed in this book will have a tremendous advantage over their competitors, and everyone gains. Customers gain because all their suppliers will really understand what they need, and deliver it rapidly in distinguishable ways. Companies gain by being more efficient and more profitable. Stakeholders gain by having their objectives met with greater rewards.

THE PRODUCT DEFINITION PROCESS

There are seven distinct steps that should be followed:

1. Know what you need to achieve (corporate direction setting);
2. Understand your market(s);
3. Define what produces quality (customer satisfaction);
4. Develop the options (different solutions, product elements or configurations);
5. Determine the value of the product elements;
6. Optimise the value and cost equation;
7. Develop the product.

This chapter provides an outline of a systematic process for developing products which focuses on the goals of the company and the requirements of the customer (steps 1 and 2). Chapter 2 expands on certain aspects of these techniques in more detail (steps 3–7).

CORPORATE DIRECTION SETTING

Products should be the end result of a logical process which starts 'at the top' and flows down through greater levels of detail to practical plans. It is not the function of this chapter to describe this process in detail, but to show its interdependence with product development.

Although the corporate direction setting process is presented here as being linear, it is in fact iterative, with each pass refining the early stages. Therefore it should be born in mind, that the mission statement, for example, does not come out of thin air, but should be based on a sound understanding of the business and its environment.

Mission

The first output from the process is normally a statement which defines the mission of the business. This *Mission Statement* should describe what the business is and what it is striving to achieve. It will normally include a broad description of the products, markets and possibly geographic coverage of the company, both at present and in the medium term.

A good mission statement will:

- help develop clear objectives and strategies;
- provide a unifying force within the company;
- show that profit is not the only goal;
- provide a sense of direction for the company;
- be a practical guide for decision making.

The mission statement says in which direction the company is going, but not the intended 'ultimate' destination. Some companies prefer to embody this in a separate statement—the company vision.

Objectives

This sense of direction and ultimate destination must then be translated into more immediate goals—the milestones along the way towards achieving them. This is the role that corporate objectives play in the planning process. The objectives should in effect be a description of what must be achieved in order to realise the company's mission (and vision). However, objectives do not flow from the mission automatically. They must be appropriate for the company and its external environment, and they *must* therefore be based on a careful appraisal of two areas: external environment analysis and internal (company) analysis.

- **External environment analysis:** The external environment is the stage on which the company acts and is subject to two main influences. *Macro-environmental forces* affect all businesses of given types—they include political, economic, social, technological, cultural and demographic forces. *Micro-environmental influences* are more specific to a given situation—they will include customers, competitors, suppliers and channels of distribution. All of these factors will have an influence on whether a company can be successful, and how it should put itself in a position to be so.

  The process whereby a company examines these external influences is known as *scanning* (see 'Techniques', on page 40 the analysis is to examine *opportunities* and *threats*. An opportunity is an area where a company can take action to enjoy some competitive advantage. To do this it must make use of its distinctive competencies (or business strengths) in a way which matches the key success requirements of the market, and in which it is better than its competitors. A threat is the reverse of this. It is some activity or trend in the external environment which will harm the company's ability to be successful, unless it is countered by deliberate action on behalf of the company.

- **Internal (company) analysis:** Opportunities and threats exist outside the company and will potentially be available to or act on all companies in a given market. To understand the company's relative ability to exploit or counter these, you need to understand the internal environment within this external context.

  The structured technique used is to examine the *strengths* and *weaknesses* of the company. These are normally relative to any given external situation, so should be carried out with reference to the opportunities defined during the external environmental analysis (scanning). Clearly a major element of this will be whether the company's resources are adequate to exploit the opportunity identified. It is particularly important to understand the skills and potential in the people employed within the company. Gaps or areas of weakness should be addressed in succession planning and selection decisions.

Having scanned and analysed the external environment and analysed the internal environment (often called a strengths, weaknesses, opportunities and threats analysis—SWOT), the company is finally in a position to formulate its objectives or goals. There are normally several sets of objectives, which should flow hierarchically, each layer being a logical derivation from those above it as well as being consistent with the SWOT results.

At the highest level one would hope to see objectives which refer to long-term market share goals, a common feature in many Japanese companies. In the West they might be more typically relating to return on capital employed. The next level would translate these into more specific goals such as increasing sales, reducing the investment base etc. Further down should be goals relating to specific markets (eg statements of target market share within individual market segments and territories), products (eg what fraction of turnover is to come from new products) and organisational changes (eg cost savings or investment targets). Most importantly, these goals have to be consistent with each other as well as consistent with the business mission and the external environment.

All these corporate objectives should be defined in three dimensions:

1. direction (eg increase or decrease);

2. amount (number of units or percentage change);

3. time (by month, quarter, year etc.).

Product and market strategies

If the role of the mission and objectives is to tell you *where* the com-

pany is going, the strategy states *how* this will be achieved. Porter*
categorises three generic types of winning strategy and shows that
firms which follow none of these (the middle-of-the-roaders) perform the worst.

- **Overall cost leadership:** The company strives to achieve the
  lowest cost of producing and distributing its products to be able
  to sell at a lower price than its competitors and hence gain a
  large market share.

- **Differentiation:** The company concentrates on producing
  products which produce some customer benefit(s) which are
  valued generally in the market and hence win a price premium
  or improved market share.

- **Focus:** The company concentrates on narrow market seg-
  ment(s) rather than the whole market. It specialises in satisfying
  the needs of its segments either through cost leadership or differentiation.

Clearly these are no more than general descriptions of type—the
actual strategy adopted will come about through programmes of
action which implement these principles. However, remembering
the lesson from Porter's study, it is only companies that concentrate
on *one* of these strategies that succeed—swapping between them at
will is not a viable option!

Knowledge of how a product is intended to compete in the above
terms should have a dramatic effect on the direction of product
development. It will define the intended market (whether this is the
whole market or a segment of it) and what qualitative position is
sought. Without this strategy it will be impossible for the development team to proceed without guesswork, and hence with a much
greater risk of failure.

As well as determining a competitive strategy, companies with
anything more than a very simple range of products will also need
to consider their product strategy.

A product strategy should follow from the above process, with
specific concentration on the company's technological and product
strengths as well as the key competitive requirements of the markets they operate in. The process will also have to examine critically
the likely development of technology and how this will be adopted
by their competitors. As a result of this process, the company
should be able to plan, in outline terms at least, how its product
range should evolve.

---

*Porter, Michael E (1980) *Competitive Strategy: Techniques for Analysing
Industries and Competitors*, The Free Press, New York.

Policy

So far discussion has concentrated on the strategic framework which corporate management needs to develop to define one dimension of the objectives of product development. However, the company has another vital role in guiding and constraining these developments. To produce a well ordered and consistent environment for product developers, the company will need to produce policies that guide the activities which need to be common between different developments. Such policies should include:*

- design (intellectual property) protection;
- product liability;
- recording design data and decisions;
- change control;
- training of development staff;
- using external resources;
- the physical development environment;
- design process evaluation;
- design verification;
- performance incentives and career paths;
- product evaluation, including third party certification or approval;
- assessing new product concepts.

Summary

Product development must take place within a framework of clear strategic thinking by senior managers in the company. If products exist to realise the company's objectives, these must be carefully formulated and communicated in a way that is genuinely useful to those responsible for product development, without imposing unnecessary constraints.

Use the following checklist at the beginning of your own product development to test if this thinking process has been carried out in your company.

1. *What is the company's mission? How will this development further this mission?*
2. *What quantified objectives must this development achieve to be successful? Do the measures include a market share target*

---

*Adapted from *BS7000: 1989 Guide to managing product design*, BSI, Park Street, London.

(as well as the more normal Return on Investment, Internal Rate of Return, Gross Margin etc. requirements). Do the objectives include a date by which they must be achieved?

3. *What market(s) is the development aimed at? Will the product address the whole market or some defined sub-sections of it (niches)? [If the latter, continue with the checklist regarding each niche separately as a complete market.]*

4. *Is the product intended to exploit a specific or unique market opportunity? What are the bounds of this (time frame, nature and price)?*

5. *What are the key success criteria in this market? Which are product related and which company related? Does the company's existing strengths match these?*

6. *How will you compete—by price leadership or by providing added value by being differentiated from competing products?*

7. *What market position is sought (eg top of the market, mid-market . . .)?*

8. *Has the competition's reaction been anticipated? Have you planned any spoiling action that should be an objective of the development (eg incremental launches, phased pricing changes)?*

9. *How will this fit into the company product strategy? (eg what product range does it fit into, what are the roll-out plans for related products and how will subsequent product development be used to manage the product lifecycle—mid-life kicks etc.)?*

10. *How have development objectives been prioritised? If three dimensions have been specified (timescale, cost and functionality), have the permitted trade-offs between them been defined?*

If you can't answer these questions really quite categorically, then you are not ready to start the product-specific development process.

MARKET FOCUS

Having defined the corporate level objectives of the development, attention can now turn to the customer in more detail. We have already established that it is vital for the end product to achieve customer satisfaction, although this is rather a passive goal. A more uplifting goal is to produce a product that will achieve widespread 'customer acclaim'—ie a positive acceptance that the product is not just good enough, but better than the alternatives. The next step then is to gain a good understanding of these customers, who they are and what factors will produce this acclaim.

There may be many routes by which a company reaches this point in product development. An entrenched company will typically be extending its range or replacing an ageing product. A company in the process of diversification may be developing completely new products for its existing customer group, or even a new product for a new (to them) market. Others may be basing the development on an invention or some breakthrough from research. This background will affect how well the company has defined its image of the product to be developed. Some may readily admit to a flawed knowledge of their customers, what they want and how to satisfy them. Others may believe they know these things perfectly.

Experience shows that companies that carry out development *without* a systematic analysis of the potential customer will miss important pointers to how they can make more successful products. Every company needs to follow a clear line of reasoning that will produce answers to the following sequence of questions:

1. Who are the customers?
2. What are their needs and wants?
3. Are they all similar in their needs and behaviour or should they be treated as distinct groups?
4. How are these needs satisfied at present?
5. How will we communicate our development to them?
6. How will they obtain and pay for our product?

The second point above is worth dwelling on briefly. It is very easy for companies with real expertise in a market and product area to believe they know what their customers need. But is this enough? What matters must be an understanding of their wants, or to introduce the terminology used extensively later: what will produce *customer value* (ie what the customer values). There will be some underlying need for each want, but not necessarily a customer want for each need as perceived by the seller. This is not to say that these needs don't exist or can't be turned into wants, simply that someone must do the work to turn a need into customer value. If the want already exists it is, to say the least, an easier target.

Only then, with an understanding of all these issues (questions 1 to 6 above), can the product be defined properly from the customer's perspective. This section will look at what information is required to answer these questions and how they can be answered. The rest of the definition process will be discussed in the next chapter.

Information requirements

Who is the customer?

If the process has been followed so far, we will already know:

- which market the product will be selling into;

- what position within the market it is intended to occupy;
- which major sub-group of potential customers it is aimed at (if the market is segmented).

For example, if we are in the business of selling cars, we might now know that we are developing one for the UK business user (a segment of the overall market) and that it will be an executive model (mid-market).

This should give us a good start in working out who it is we actually have to sell to, but it does not in itself provide the answer. In the above example, for instance, is the end user the only one whose needs we must satisfy in order to produce a good car? Clearly not, because the decision to purchase a particular model will be influenced (if not actually made) by a group of people, including those who:

- provide the money (eg the user's boss);
- determine company buying policy and supplier relationships;
- are concerned with projecting a particular image of the company;
- provide peer group pressure;
- maintain and service it.

In many buying decisions, the decision making unit (or DMU—those who have direct influence over what to buy) is made up of a number of people, and may be influenced by people outside this group. These others have no direct control, but can sway one or more of the DMU, eg a respected journalist who can review the product. Each of these people may have a slightly (or even dramatically) different perspective on what makes a good product.

In some markets the situation can be even more complicated than this. In the case of many consumer goods, the end user will buy what the retailer stocks. If it is essential for the product to be available in retail outlets, it may turn out that convincing the retailer to stock it, particularly when he or she will only carry one line, is most of the battle. Clearly, you must also be able to convince the end purchaser, otherwise the retailer will de-list the product.

An example of this occurred recently. In the UK there is a large market for child safety gates (often referred to as stairgates), the majority of which are sold by retail chains. The technology of manufacturing these gates is relatively cheap and the main barrier to entering this market is gaining retail acceptance. An enterprising company wishing to enter this market concluded that, as retail space is always at a premium and these gates are bulky to store and display, they could steal a march on the competition by launching a self-assembly gate taking up a fraction of the normal pack size. This did in fact have the desired effect—at first. Many retailers stocked it with willingness, but were then disappointed to find that it did not sell. Subsequent research has shown that mums (who are predominantly responsible for these purchases), simply could not believe that a gate that they could assemble easily would really be strong and safe enough to stop their children falling down stairs!

This illustrates a general point: unless you sell direct to the end users, you will also have to 'sell to' those people responsible for the product reaching them—the distribution channel.

If you want to be sure of the eventual success of your product, you must at least consider the differing needs of all of these groups of people. Ultimately, the one whose needs matter most is normally the end user. However, this must not blind you to the need to consider the requirements of the DMU, the distribution channel and others who may influence the eventual purchase.

In the process of product development there is another type of 'customer' to consider. These are people who receive the output of your efforts more directly and will judge you on its quality, based on their own criteria. This group will include others within the development team, suppliers, and others outside the team but within the company. This is the extended team (see Chapter 4). The first of these is fairly obvious and most well-run teams will communicate well enough for the needs of the person receiving your direct work to be clear. Suppliers (eg the manufacturer who produces your product) should in most instances be regarded as part of the team (see Chapter 5), but will certainly need to accept your work and be able to use it. They will therefore impose certain constraints on the detail of what you produce (the interface between development and manufacture/supply).

The group of 'internal customers' described above may actually turn out to have more immediate impact on you as a product development team than the ones that really matter (the end customers). This is because they will be trying to judge your performance at various stages *before* success in the market (the only true and accurate gauge) can be measured. You should therefore take special care to consider their needs and to involve them (see also Chapter 4—responsibility charting).

What are their needs and wants?

Before considering this point, we must assume that the company knows roughly what product it is to develop—a straightforward process for companies established in a product area. For those diversifying into a new area to be able to specify this (approximately at least), they must first carry out a matching process between their strengths and the market's requirements.

Generally this knowledge of 'roughly what the product is' is only the starting point for a detailed study of the customer's requirements. The resulting description of the product concept may be quite different, because it is based on a thorough understanding of the customer, rather than just an opinion.

To illustrate this we will consider the recent development of a 'sunburn avoidance device'. Market research (scanning) had highlighted the increasing concern many consumers (and the media) were voicing about skin damage caused by over exposure to the sun. At the same time, medical research was showing a link between sunburn and skin cancer in later life. It was suggested that that this increased concern might give an opportunity for a product that measures the harmful rays from the sun and warns the user at some limit. The initial concept for this product was very simple—it was to measure the radiation and sound an alarm when the total exposure reached a limit based on the user's skin type. However, a more detailed consideration of the users' needs showed that the real requirement was for functions that allowed some form of 'time management'. Thus the key function of the product that was then developed was a prediction of how long they could safely stay in the sun, not simply measurement and alarm.

It is clearly important to define the central function of the product that is to be developed, but even this misses the point of being customer focused. As was discussed in the introduction, the reason for developing a product is to exchange it for your customers' money. This is an exchange of one thing they value (money) with another (your product). For the product to be valued by them it must give them some benefit(s). Thus the question should be *what customer benefit does the product offer*, rather than its functions or features. In the above example the core benefit became 'managing your time to avoid sunburn'.

It is important to define this core benefit for two reasons. First, it is the *core benefit* that needs to be communicated to the potential purchasers. This is dealt with more fully later. Secondly, it allows you to define the *total potential market* for the product. This is the group of customers who share the same need (or desire), and this may well include customers who are outside the target market for the development. If this occurs it is certainly worth re-examining the basis on which the target market was selected to see if the potential opportunity is larger than originally expected. It does not necessarily mean however that a product should be developed to try to satisfy all the potential market, for reasons given later.

As has been stated, the core benefit is the central thing the product provides. However, it is not the only aspect of the product that must be developed. The product which provides real utility is packaged, styled, may have many features etc. This is referred to as *The Total Product* (Figure 1.5).

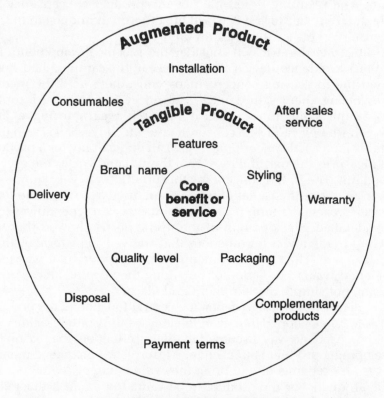

Figure 1.5 The total product

Whilst not all of these aspects are necessarily present in all products, it is surprising how few of them are considered at all during the course of conventional product development.

The adoption of this customer focused view of the product forces developers to see the wider needs of their market and hence how vital a multi-disciplinary team is during development. The package that makes up the total customer benefit can be fluid, and issues that may well be needs (that are not valued) at one stage become important wants later. For example, in the world of car safety, ABS and air-bags were luxuries that few would pay for a few years ago. Changing perceptions and expectations (helped along by the marketing communications of the pioneering manufacturers!) have led to them being demanded and valued by increasing numbers of car buyers today.

Segmentation

Having determined who the customers are and what benefits the product will offer, we can now start to consider whether one product alone will meet their requirements. Classically markets are segmented (ie sub-divided into homogenous groups) based on demographic or lifestyle criteria. These criteria are determined primarily for communications and selling activity, and may not necessarily be useful in product development terms. For this, we need to know what groupings exist that are homogenous in their requirements from products. This is a complex issue which must be dealt with in stages. The first can be looked at now, but the final view of product-centred segmentation must wait until later in the definition process, when we can measure customer reactions to product features.

At this stage, we need to determine how the product will be used (what usage types and occasions exist), and make an outline judgement on the relative value placed on the main product benefit in each of these types of use. To use the example of child safety gates mentioned earlier, although all are used as barriers to prevent children from some hazard (nearly all—some are actually used to prevent pets from getting into the wrong part of the house!), there are several distinctly different situations (usage types) in which they are used. Most are used either at the top or bottom of a staircase, but appreciable numbers are used in doorways or corridors to prevent egress from bedrooms or access to the kitchen. The different requirements placed on the product by these different usage types are significant (eg a trip hazard caused by the gate is more significant at the top of the stairs than elsewhere).

Recognising these different usage types and occasions is important because it allows you to segment the market in a way that is significant in product development terms. When you look at what features to build in and where to spend the development effort, you need to be able to examine information from the market to uncover these differences. For example, there are two types of safety gate, those with a frame plus an opening section (and hence a bottom bar which could form a trip hazard), and those that hinge directly from the wall (with no frame and bottom bar). If we assessed the attitude of our target market towards the trip hazard without segmenting by location, we could find that the *average* attitude is neutral (about one third are used at the top of the stairs), but this would mask the fact that two groups exist, and in reality there might be a market for two types of gates, or a new format that could satisfy both situations.

Competitors and substitutes

We also need to know how the potential customers satisfy their requirements at present. This is an activity which overlaps greatly with the first level of segmentation as, although one can speculate that different usage types and occasions may exist, the existence of different means of satisfying the core need can provide the required proof.

Assuming that we have identified the customer group we are aiming our development at, and the core benefit we have identified is real and not imagined, the customers can behave in one of three possible ways:

1. They may buy products of the type you are planning to develop.
2. They may find the cost of these outweighs their benefits and buy nothing.
3. They may find some other means of providing the benefits, possibly using a substitute product.

Clearly each of these outcomes is important, because your product will only sell if they follow the first course *and* choose your product over all existing ones. Most companies, therefore, will have a look at what the direct competition is offering; few will see that they are also 'competing' against completely different classes of products.

An important part of the definition process must be to investigate all these products (competitive and substitute) and to make sure that the planned development will be competitive in this wider context by offering benefits that are valued more than the cost of the product, and more than other solutions to their needs.

Communications requirements

It is not normally part of the product development process to determine how the existence and benefits of the product will eventually be communicated to the market. However, product developers must be aware that this communications process is going to be vital to the ultimate success of the product. It will almost certainly have an effect on the tangible or augmented product to be developed. Due consideration of this must be made sufficiently early in the development such that any consequences can be incorporated without loss of efficiency or reducing time to market.

The clearest examples of this are to be found most often in consumer markets, particularly where advertising is the key means of communication. In most forms of consumer advertising the message must be clear and simple to be effective, otherwise informing the market about the benefits of your product will not work. Thus, when Sir Clive Sinclair launched his C5 (a small electric vehicle intended for commuting and about-town use), he was unable to convince consumers through national advertising that the vehicle was safe. Had the vehicle been aimed at a small, easily reached group (golfers?), he could have overcome such fears through more targeted advertising and editorial coverage in specialist media, where readers might be expected to absorb more complex messages. Conversely, knowing and understanding the limited abilities of available mass communications media should have had a big impact on the development of the product itself. For example, safety features could have been given a higher priority, both in development and communications.

At an early stage of development, it is therefore necessary to establish that you will be able to:

1. Communicate the benefits of the product in a way that is meaningful and credible to the customer.
2. Use channels of communication that are both cost effective and capable of delivering the required messages.

It is good practice to establish early in development (at the concept stage) what this message will be and how it will be delivered. You can then refer back to this regularly during development to test whether the product still fits the selling message or, if this needs to be changed, that it is still credible and the medium of communications will support it.

Distribution implications

The same attention must be paid to the means of physically getting your product into the hands of your customers and how this could influence product development. An example of this is given earlier in this chapter (page 33), where an extreme view of the retailer's requirements of the product determined the product format (self-assembly for reduced shelf space). Other, more subtle, examples occur regularly, where pack sizes and the sub-division of multi-part products (eg personal computers) are chosen to optimise warehouse space or pallet packing density. The exact configuration of a pack can also be influenced by the need to adjust last minute options (eg country specific software and keyboard overlays for PCs).

The implications that should be considered include:

• how installation and after-sales support will be provided—what level of maintenance and repair skills the product demands;

• the need for adjusting last-minute options (colour, language etc.) and where this will be done (own warehouse, distributor, retailer);

- the number and sizes of packed units:
  - —how they will be handled and by whom (check regulations on manual lifting);
  - —how they will be bulk-packed and transported. Whether the aspect ratio of the pack(s) will affect the efficiency of this;

- legislative or user pressure to recycle packing by return or public recycling facilities;

- other elements of the product which might require careful disposal or recycling (eg batteries containing heavy metal compounds)—how these will be handled.

Techniques

In the last section we considered the nature of the information needed about the customers and their requirements, but not how to gather it. It is impossible to be definitive about the techniques to be used for this as each company, and even each project, will find itself in slightly different circumstances which will determine the most appropriate mix of information gathering activities. The techniques presented here form the framework which has been found useful in widely differing circumstances, but which must be adapted according to the limitations of available resource and the detail of the information required.

These techniques, which are all types of market research, are discussed here only in the context of the information needs outlined above. Clearly this is not intended to be an exhaustive discussion of the whole topic of market research, but more a guide to the sort of techniques that a development team may well have to employ themselves.

Familiarisation

A vital first stage that can greatly increase the efficiency of all subsequent research is simply to become familiar with the market. Most people tasked with this research might be expected to have sufficient outline knowledge of the market, but particularly during diversification into new markets (and even for completely new products into existing markets) and when a new team is tackling the subject, it is worth pausing before commencing the detailed research to make sure you understand the terms used: the key words and concepts that can be used to approach the subject. This can often be done during a briefing session with someone else in the company who has *recent* knowledge of the target market (and application) or by reading recent relevant journals or articles.

However it is important not to 'waste' the goodwill of a key information source at this stage. If you can't find a suitable source who is easily, preferably casually, approached for some outline information, don't be tempted to interview a guru on the subject until your grasp of it is sufficient to make the interview really effective.

The information you need at this stage is:

- a starter list of useful information sources (people, companies and journals);

- a starter list of key words which will lead to the information you require;

- some understanding of the terms you will come across;

- major operators in the market who need to be researched.

Desk research

The next step is to gain the most detailed understanding possible (and appropriate) of the target market and application. The purpose behind this is to make the best possible use of any subsequent research, bearing in mind that the next stages can be relatively expensive. Fortunately information technology has enabled some efficient and low cost means of gathering information which can greatly enhance subsequent research, making the whole research phase very cost effective.

It should be remembered that there are two strands to this information gathering process:

1. information about the market; and
2. information about competitive and substitute products.

The strands are not separate; information from the market will give clues as to who the competitors (of both types) are, and information about competitive products and companies may well open out the market search area.

The first task is to obtain product and company literature identified during the familiarisation stage. This should be read carefully and classified. At this stage any classification will obviously be rough or even wrong, but it can be refined later, as long as the information is not lost at this stage! If possible and appropriate, visits to trade fairs and seminars can also yield valuable information. The main activity, however, is to understand what is going on in the market—in the past, now, and what is expected in the future. Desk research means using published information sources to obtain data. Fortunately, almost every market gets written about by someone, somewhere; this may be in daily newspapers, popular journals, specialist journals and newsletters, consumer reports or even published pieces of market research! The problem lies in how easy this information is to find in the area in which you are interested.

In recent years increasing use has been made of the online electronic databases as the most efficient source for this type of information. There are a variety of databases available from a number of database providers who are accessed using a personal computer or terminal via several database hosts.

A *database provider* is a company that gathers information from a number of sources (journals, patents, product announcements etc.). They may obtain this information in electronic format directly from the publisher, or they may have to re-type it into a computer, but ultimately it ends up in electronic form. This is then given some structure, usually unique to that provider, and indexed. The structure allows certain types of information to be searched (such as journal title, date of publication, language or body text) and the indexing allows the data to be found rapidly. Some providers will allocate index codes (or keywords) to the database to allow searching by subject. In this way, records relating to a particular subject can be found even if they don't mention an obvious keyword in the text itself.

Some database providers make available a number of separate *databases*. Each database will cover information of a particular type, structured in the same way. Thus a single provider may have databases covering general market intelligence, new product announcements, specialist newsletters and files covering specific industries such as computing. Other providers have databases containing indices of all granted patents, published market research reports etc.

A *database host* provides the means by which you access these databases. Using a computer (personal or dumb terminal) and a modem, you dial into the host (using an account code and password to identify who the bill should be sent to) and select which database (or which clusters of databases, as some allow you to search more than one at once) you wish to use. Some provide facilities that allow you to see which databases are appropriate by listing the number of records in each that relate to the subject you are interested in. The exact mechanism you use to access the information you need will vary from host to host, and sometimes even between different database providers. Most 'search languages' are fairly easy to learn, but care must be taken to ensure that you are finding directly relevant records, otherwise the cost effectiveness of the method can be lost. Most hosts will charge you based on a combination of the time you are connected to each database plus the amount of information you display or print.

It is very likely that your knowledge will mature during research, and you may not be aware at first of the relevance of some of the information you gather. It is therefore always advisable to keep a log (or 'download') file of the information you uncover. You must be aware of copyright requirements, which generally allow you to take an electronic record for your own use for a single particular purpose but not for dissemination or re-use.

These files may be usefully edited (getting rid of spurious communications details and records that are clearly not relevant), then added to the information uncovered in subsequent research (interviews etc.). Thus a single reference data source is generated from which to draw the information needed. Most of the functions required for this can be obtained from the searching facilities of text editors or from more powerful free-form database packages.*

To be useful, the information gathered must be organised. A useful technique is to scan it first for topics of interest (eg competitors, market share, market forecasts, segmentation indicators, industry structure, contacts and other information sources etc.). References to these are then compiled into separate lists. As the research proceeds these lists can then be kept up-to-date, thus forming a 'moving picture' of the market which gets more accurate as your information becomes more complete.

Interviews

The next step is to gather 'primary' information, ie directly from the various customers (as defined earlier). Up to this point the information that has been gathered is classed as secondary—ie gathered by others and summarised, paraphrased or interpreted before being included in some published source. Whilst it is important to have the understanding and overview of the subject that this can provide, it must be regarded as supplementary to primary research. One of the main reasons for this is the question of interpretation. All data is interpreted and filtered before being reported, and the chances that the publication contains the particular interpretation you need are normally very slim. This is often most true in published market research reports, where even understanding how the authors have defined the scope of a market, let alone how they have measured its size, can be an impossible task.

What is required then is at least some (and maybe a great deal) of information directly from your target market. Referring back to the section 'Who is the customer?', we can see that the composition of this group can be complex, and include:

- end users;

- the wider decision-making unit;

- the distribution chain (dealers, retailers);

- journalists.

*For example, *Info Select* from Micro Logic, Hackensack NJ, USA.

Because of this, you should consider whether you need to gather information directly from any or all of these groups. To be cost effective, it is always worth starting at the end of this list and working back to the end user. Thus journalists and distributors can act as a useful information focus—but bear in mind that they are *not* the end customer and will put their own perspective on the information they give you.

Whoever you intend to gather this data from, you must be well organised, so:

1. Define what you need to achieve.
2. List the key topics which will uncover the information.
3. Decide how you will collect (telephone or face-to-face), organise and analyse the data.
4. From your knowledge of how the market is segmented, decide how many to interview and from which groups.
5. Write the questionnaire or topic script that will be used to structure the interviews.
6. Test the procedure on a small sample first.

Structured interviews carried out within the above structure can be very effective in gathering information about market size, shares, trends, buying behaviour, composition of the DMU, key purchase criteria, requirements of the total product and so on. Unless carried out with a great deal of skill, they are not very good at exploring issues relating to new or unfamiliar products. They can also be a very expensive way of gathering information, and in many circumstances are best used sparingly to test tentative conclusions formed during desk research. Effective communications, dealt with in Chapter 5, will help make the best use of these interviews.

Groups

Another technique used widely during product development is the use of focus groups. These are small groups (usually about a dozen) of potential purchasers or existing users who are recruited to match some sub-set of the target market. Thus several separate groups may be held, each containing those representing one way of segmenting the market. They are brought together for a structured discussion (usually led by a moderator). This technique may be used to explore the needs surrounding potential product opportunity, or more specifically to test their reaction to a proposed product compared to existing or alternative products.

Care must be taken during recruitment and especially in running the group. Outspoken people with strong personalities can influence the results if the session is not properly designed. Possible bias may also have to be taken into account in the interpretation of the results. Depending on the precise objectives of the groups, it may also be possible to get respondents to complete simple questionnaires individually after the group discussion has taken place and issues are fresh in their minds. This can often illuminate the bias that 'group think' can introduce (see Chapter 5).

The direct results from groups are qualitative, that is the verbal comments and suggestions made by the group are collected and analysed by the researcher. It is therefore vital that he or she understands exactly what information is pertinent to the product development being undertaken. Ideally you should use someone from within the company to run such groups, someone who is not closely involved with the project (to avoid bias), but who must understand all the issues. This required combination of excellent interpersonal skills together with the marketing and, possibly, technical understanding, may necessitate the use of external researchers, who must then be effectively integrated into the team.

Other techniques

Direct observation can be a very useful way of discovering how products are actually used, and what the problems are. It is a technique increasingly used in the computer industry, where products can now be configured to gather their own usage data as well as to record problems and comments from users. It can also provide some useful insights where a product is used by a number of people at roughly the same time, eg children's play equipment or in the classroom.

Hall tests are used to measure consumers' responses to new products, usually whilst they are shopping. They may be shown a video of the product in use, a mocked-up advert or a model of the product and they will be asked a number of questions about their reactions.

Conjoint research is discussed more fully in the next chapter as it forms the backbone of the product optimisation method. It is a technique for measuring the relative importance of individual aspects of a product and the value of certain options. It can be used in the course of most of the primary research techniques discussed in this section.

Organisation

Although this information gathering process may seem to be highly specialised to some companies, normally performed outside the normal scope of a development project (if at all), it is vital to the success of this integrated approach that it is carried out by resources who are regarded as part of the product development process and part of the development team. This does not necessarily mean that a team of engineers must suddenly acquire these market research skills (although that is one good solution), or that skilled external resources such as consultants or market research companies must not be used. What it does mean is that *whoever* carries out the work must be part of the team (see Chapter 4). Traditionally they may commence this work before a formal product team is formed, in which case they should become the kernel of this nascent team, ensuring that not only the data is passed on, but also the understanding and the circumstances that make the information meaningful.

Summary

We have discussed the nature of the information required in order to give a useful market focus to the development goals, and have suggested six areas of information that will be required:

1. Who the customer is.
2. The customers' needs and wants.
3. How the customers can be grouped to form homogenous market segments.
4. What companies and products will compete directly and indirectly.
5. How the requirements of communications will affect the nature of the product.
6. How the requirements of distribution and selling will affect the nature of the product.

To gather this information we have discussed a framework for research specific to the requirements of product development:

- **Secondary information**
  - —Familiarisation reading and meetings
  - —Desk research
  - —Information organisation
  - —Forming a framework for primary research.

- **Primary information**
  - —Interviews
  - —Research groups
  - —Analysis.

2
The Goal—
Quality and Function

One of the largest sources of conflict during development is differing views on exactly what the product should be. It seems to be something on which everyone has a valid opinion—marketing 'know their customers', R&D understand the forces of competing technologies, stylists know about new design solutions, manufacturing know what can be made well. This can lead to enormous amounts of time wasting argument, with each camp sure of their ground—after all, they *are* the experts in their area, and no-one can deny that their area is important. All too often, what eventually does get developed will depend on the opinion of the group (or person) with the greatest political power in the company.

To avoid this you need the wholehearted acceptance by everyone involved that there is only one important goal: to achieve customer satisfaction with a sensible cost structure, and hence profitable sales. What is then needed is the acceptance of some *method* which will define successful products and take into account the valuable inputs from all parts of the company that have a valid contribution to make.

The need for a generally accepted method must be stressed. Unless there is a system which is both accepted and visible, the danger of lapsing into product definition by force of opinion is too great.

How can this be achieved? If we accept that satisfying the customer is paramount, and that the marketing department is closest to the customers, can't we just accept their opinion? The answer to this should be a qualified *no*, because the best product comes from the *creative* compromise between what the customers want and what the company can devise. Successful products will therefore depend on the performance of all groups within the company who can make a valuable contribution. Obviously this will include marketing and sales, but also technical R&D, manufacturing, styling, service and support, buying etc., plus (increasingly) the environmental lobby. What is required is a multi-disciplinary approach that is focused first and foremost on the customer, but also builds on the best knowledge from other parts of the company.

One technique has been developed and used to dramatic effect by many Japanese companies. Known as Quality Function Deployment (QFD), it has grown out of total quality management techniques. The rather awkward term derives from the idea that quality means producing customer satisfaction, and the job of product development is to create (or 'deploy') product functions in order to create quality. Given the success of the technique, it is surprising how little it seems to be practised in the West. There are probably many reasons why this is so, but there are two main issues. The first of these is cultural. Apart from a traditional lack of democratic procedures in Western companies (QFD requires multi-disciplinary teams which run democratically), Western teams involved in NPD seem to avoid the rigorous mental discipline and attention to fine detail that the Japanese exhibit. An understanding of the natural roles people play within teams, and especially the characteristics of implementers and completer-finishers (see Chapter 4), will help overcome this.

The second issue is that the technique, as conventionally described, lacks certain key inputs. The missing inputs are:

1. the determination of corporate and marketing objectives as part of the process of defining the product;
2. the methods needed to research what defines quality;
3. the techniques for optimising the balance between customer value and the cost of providing it.

Although QFD is an important and valuable technique, it is only one stage in a broader product definition process that also overcomes the above shortcomings.

Four main stages of the definition process emerge:

*   company and marketing objective setting;
*   gathering specific customer information;
*   quality function deployment;
*   measuring customer value and trading it off against product and development cost.

So far in this description of the rational product definition process we have concentrated on the first two of these: the techniques for defining corporate and marketing strategies, and the preliminary information required from and about the target customers. What follows draws heavily from the technique of Quality Function Deployment, but is not a definition of QFD. An authoritative description of QFD is covered by way of detailed case studies in a book of the same title,* which also shows how the technique can provide a means of measuring quality during production.

DEFINING QUALITY

If the goal is to develop a product that will produce customer satisfaction, there can be only one place to start the detailed product definition—with the customer. The last section dealt in some detail with the process of gaining an understanding of who the customers are and what their needs are. We have stressed the need to research the customer directly (once you have sufficient understanding of the market to allow effective research) for one very good reason: we must start with the customers' own perceptions of their needs before we can develop a product to satisfy them.

This works well when the customers know they have a need and try to satisfy it already. However, there is an increasing trend for new legislation or new technology to produce opportunities for products for which customers have no perceived need. This may be to satisfy legislation (eg on environmental protection), or because technology enables a solution to something that customers do not traditionally seek to solve, because the problem has previously just been accepted or solved by completely different means. When such circumstances arise, these techniques can still be used, but they must be preceded by educating a representative customer group to enable you to satisfy them—not just the legislators or the inventors!

Quality Function Deployment starts with the customers' descriptions of their needs and produces an understanding of how the functions and features of a product map onto them. Throughout this chapter we will refer to the hypothetical case of a bedside alarm clock.

Customer verbatims (statements)

The first step is to collect together all the information you have about the needs of your customers. It is important that this must be:

1. collected directly from end users (and other members of the purchase decision making unit if applicable);
2. statements of need and want *in their own words*;
3. restricted to *their* understanding of the benefits they seek; and
4. kept separate from any descriptions of how they think the benefits should be provided.

*Akao, Yoji (1990) *Quality Function Deployment*, Productivity Press, Cambridge, Mass.

The last two points are important. In many markets customers have become expert in the technology of the product they buy. Asking the wrong questions will only elicit a description of their view of how you should design the product. Your task is to understand what their real needs are, in order that you can use your development team's creativity to provide solutions that will give you an overall competitive advantage. Rarely will the customers be knowledgeable enough to do this for you (or if they are, you should recruit them into the team!).

In some markets, notably for high-tech products, getting this right is essential to the success of the process. This may involve taking a highly critical approach to gathering these customer verbatims. If the customers have become indoctrinated by the technology and solutions, eg by competitors or by specialist publications, you will have to work hard to 'peel away' their layers of assumptions to reveal their underlying needs. For example, if customers are discussing their need for an audible alarm to wake them up, statements of need such as 'I need an alarm intensity of 20dbB' should be rejected. Acceptable statements would include 'loud enough to wake me up', 'adjustable intensity, but gets louder if I go back to sleep'.

The importance of well run focus groups and in-depth interviews described in the last section now becomes obvious. If these have been carried out well, you should have a wealth of information from your target customers about the benefits they seek in the product area you are developing.

These are not the only sources of data. If you are already trading in similar products, it is very easy to include customer questionnaires (if there is an incentive for them to be returned) that can provide another valuable source of data. Exhibitions can also be turned into a useful source by the use of similar questionnaires. In short, every opportunity should be taken to gather such information directly from existing or targeted users. Whatever technique is used, you *must* be aware of possible bias. Traditionally only very small numbers of customers return questionnaires, and those that do are often trying to make a point. The use of competitions or random prize awards might be a low cost way of increasing the representation from this source.

For our alarm clock example, the customer verbatims may include:

> It must be easy to read the time.
> It must wake me up effectively.
> It must be easy to set the alarm.
> It must not take up too much space.

and so on.

Demanded quality items

Customers statements of sought benefits are often complex and can carry many meanings. The next task, therefore, is to extract single meaning statements from the original verbatims. This is a task for the team, not the customer, because the members of the team who have been involved with the research into the customer so far should now have a good understanding of the application and the wealth of data from research.

Re-word the original customer statements into ones that carry a single meaning. These too may sometimes appear to have more than one implication, so a third level of benefit should be added, one which must be implied in order for the stated requirement to be true. The aim throughout is to concentrate on the benefits sought, and not to be distracted into thinking about solutions at this stage. You will thus end up with a hierarchy of:

- **sought benefit as stated (complex)**

- statements of individual sought benefit (several)

- *implied benefits (possibly several)*

which can be organised into groups with common themes. These often form around the original statements of need and benefit, although in some cases other ways of organising the data might be more relevant. For example, expanding some of the above statements for the alarm clock might give:

It must be easy to read the time:
    easy to see the display
        can be easily read at night
        can be read during day
        clear when read from close-up
        can be read from a distance
    easily understood display

etc.

It must wake me up effectively:
    effective intrusion into sleep
        loud enough to wake me
        doesn't wake others (in other rooms?)
    easy to silence alarm
        switch easy to find
        switch easy to operate
    wakes me if I drift off again

etc.

Quality characteristics

We are now ready to move on from an examination of benefits to determine the characteristics of the product that provides them. This is also a team activity. If the team does not already contain technical specialists, it must now be enlarged to include members who understand all tangible aspects of the product.

Quality characteristics are those aspects of the product that provide, influence or detract from all the demanded quality items listed earlier. The technique for generating the list therefore starts with the demanded quality chart. Examining each quality item in turn, you should list those features and attributes of the product that are linked to them. This will not be a one-to-one mapping; the same product attributes will often be suggested by more than one sought benefit and vice versa.

These quality characteristics will also need to be organised, often along the lines of the design architecture of the product itself. Thus for a computing product, characteristics may be grouped under electronic, mechanical, software, documentation and packaging. The level of detail that is gone into at this stage will vary according to circumstances. The first time QFD is used on a product class, the characteristics examined can be at the highest level of design architecture, with finer detail being added later. For example, starting with consideration of the 'easy to read the time' benefit, characteristics that might be suggested would include:

Time display:
 type (analogue/digital etc.)
  typeface of characters used
  alarm on indication
  alarm time indication
 size
  size of overall display area
  size of characters
  size of hands (analogue only)
 visibility
  colour of display
  colour of background
  reflectivity of display
  reflectivity of background
  contrast ratio display to background
 illumination
  light source
  power source

etc.

The QFD chart

We now have the basis of the core tool of Quality Function Deployment—the QFD chart (table 2.1). This is a matrix that shows the linkage between demanded quality and product attributes. Its power lies in the fact that it graphically represents the complex linkage between the product itself and the benefits it exists to create.

To create the chart, it is conventional to list the demanded quality items vertically on the left and the product characteristics horizontally across the top. Each cell in the matrix represents a possible relationship between a benefit and a product characteristic. The team must now determine the nature of each linkage. It is normal to characterise these as strong, medium and weak. Sometimes it is also necessary to show that a linkage can be negative as well as positive—ie a product attribute that provides certain benefits may actually detract from others. For example, the power supply needed to illuminate an alarm clock at night detracts from its overall size and portability. The cells should therefore, where necessary, show the direction of each linkage as well as its strength.

At the end of this stage you should have a graphic representation that shows how customer requirements (demanded quality items) are translated into the engineering and design language used in your company (quality characteristics). If this has been correctly constructed, anyone in the team should be able to refer to it at any stage during development. It shows exactly how any aspect of the product being developed relates to the customers' sought benefits, even though these aspects have become defined in technical terms which may mean nothing to the end user.

So far the QFD chart has allowed us to translate customer language into company-specific technical language, but it has not provided us with a means of determining what should be developed and what the priorities should be. Unless a way of doing this is found, two serious problems will arise:

1. Resource might be wasted on developments which provide no competitive advantage;
2. The need for multiple solutions might be overlooked.

This last point is not always obvious. It can happen whenever demanded quality items are in conflict, ie when any possible product attribute that could provide one demanded benefit prevents the provision of another. The above example of an alarm clock illustrates this: the means of satisfying the demand for 'can be clearly and easily read at night' (eg a lit display requiring mains power) contradicts the demand for 'small and portable'. You therefore need to know the relative importance of each sought benefit and the relative performance of existing solutions.

Function characteristic → details	TIME DISPLAY — type: typeface	alarm time indication	alarm on indication	size: display area	character size	hands size	visibility: display colour	display reflectivity	background colour	background reflectivity	contrast ratio	illumination: light type	power source	etc.	ALARM: high volume	low volume	adjustable	Relative importance	Existing product	Competitor A	Competitor B
Easy to read time — easy to see display																					
easy to read at night	⊠	×		⊠	⊠	⊠					⊠	⊠						8	1	5	9
easy to read in day	⊠	✓	✓	⊠			⊠	⊠	⊠	⊠	⊠							9	10	4	9
clear close-up		✓										✓						5	9	2	6
read from distance	⊠			⊠				⊠		⊠	⊠							3	9	1	3
read from angle	✓										⊠							2	1	1	3
Wakes me up — effective intrusion																					
loud enough												⊠			✓	×		9	7	9	5
not too loud															×	✓	✓	7	1	9	5
easy to silence																					
switch easy to find												✓					✓	10	5	2	10
switch easy to use																		7	5	2	9
General purpose																					
good for bedside use				×									⊠		✓	×	✓	10	7	4	8
good travel alarm																		5	1	9	1

Key

⊠	strong negative
×	weak negative
✓	positive
⊠	strong positive

Relative importance of quality items

Well planned research leading to the construction of the QFD chart will have given you enough information to assess the relative importance of each demanded quality item. This can, for example, be done quite simply by counting the number of times each one has been mentioned as important during groups or interviews. You may then choose to weight the responses according to the source (eg end users may be weighted more than distributors) before ranking them.

This information will be more reliable if gathered using quantitative research. This can range from simple questionnaires filled in during interviews and groups or exhibitions, through telephone research and 'omnibus studies' (where you can have a small number of questions added to a syndicated field study), to full bespoke field studies (telephone, face-to-face or postal). The technique used will depend on budget, how much information is already known and the complexity of the product. Whichever technique is chosen, be sure to rank (or rate) the sought benefits, and *not* the solutions.

Competitive evaluation

Whilst the above research is going on you should also find out how various key competitor products are rated against each of the demanded benefits. The final questionnaire (if this is the technique used) might then look like this:

Thank you for agreeing to help us design alarm clocks more suited to your needs. We need to know how important various factors are when you are buying an alarm clock. Below we list the most common customer requirements. Please tell us how important each one is to you, and how good your current alarm clock is against each factor.

Your age: **Sex:**   **Occupation:**

Make and model of your current alarm clock:
Please ring the right number below:

	5 = v.important, 1 = v. unimportant *Importance*	5 = v.good, 1 = v.bad How good your existing one is
Factor		
It should be easy to read the time	5 4 3 2 1	5 4 3 2 1
It must wake me up effectively etc.	5 4 3 2 1	5 4 3 2 1

Figure 2.1 Sample questionnaire

From this you can generate 'benchmarks' for each area of demanded quality. The leading brand or product in each area will thus be determined and this becomes the basis for comparison during development.

The need for segmentation

One way of handling the data gained from assessing relative importance and performance in each of the demanded quality areas is simply to summarise it, to produce an average response from the population sampled. However this can lead to a potentially serious problem.

We have already discussed how most large groups of customers contain sub-groups with differing needs. A random sample of potential purchasers of alarm clocks may, for example, produce the following data when averaged over the whole group:

Factor	Relative importance
1. Easy to read display	0.8
2. Small, portable	0.5
3. Easy to silence alarm	0.3

If this data actually came from a sample of respondents like these:

Response	Factor 1 Easy to read display	Factor 2 Small, portable	Factor 3 Easy to silence alarm
1	0.5	1	0.1
2	1.0	0.1	0.4
3	0.7	0.7	0.4
4	0.9	0.2	0.5
5	0.8	0.5	0.3
6	1.0	0.9	0.3
7	0.8	0.3	0.2
8	0.7	0.8	0.4
9	0.9	0.2	0.1
10	1.0	0.4	0.5

Examination will show that on factor 2 (small, portable) there are two main groups of customers, one ranking it lower than the other two factors shown, the other higher. If this were not discovered, then the company might put most of its resource into developing easy-to-read displays, and miss the fact that there are two distinct markets (in this hypothetical example), one for portable alarm clocks, the other for easily read alarms clocks, where the purchaser might be expected to trade an easy-to-read display for increased portability.

This is a simple example for the sake of clarity. In reality the techniques needed for uncovering possible sub-groups in potential buying behaviour can be complex. Generically the technique is called *cluster analysis*, and although powerful software tools* are available to carry this out (on anything but trivial examples), great care is also required in the interpretation. The software may generate measures of statistical similarity within each cluster, but this may not necessarily have any meaning in the real world.

This is another reason why it is so important to gain a detailed understanding of the market and the competition—you will need to be able to check if the segments uncovered by cluster analysis make sense. If (as in the above example, travel alarms vs. bedside alarms) the clusters found relate to known differences in buying behaviour (eg by different classes of products being bought) this is comforting.

On the other hand, if the results do *not* conform to your knowledge of the market, you may need to find other ways of clustering the data (eg using factors that are more effective), or you may need to adjust your view of the market. This latter course should only be taken if you have corroborating evidence, which could come from trade-off research. This will be described more fully later, but in this context, conjoint analysis could be used to test the hypothesis that some features are valued in combination by certain segments of the market.

Identifying competitive areas

We finally have all the information needed to determine what aspects of the product should be prioritised and what are the targets to aim for in each area of benefit. We will have by now:

- A list of the benefits demanded by the target market.

- Unambiguous statements of individual sought benefit implied by these.

- The relative importance of each of these sought benefits.

- An understanding of whether the market is segmented, and if so the size of each and the relative importances within each one.

- A full understanding of which aspects of the physical product influence each of the sought benefits.

---

*For example, SPSS, SPSS Inc., Chicago, USA.

- An understanding of the potential conflicts between enhancing certain benefits but reducing others.

- Knowledge of how competitive products measure up to customer requirements and hence a basis for comparing your product.

We can now determine which areas of the product to develop. These will be areas:

1. that the target market (or a sufficiently large segment of it) values highly;
2. that match the marketing objectives determined earlier;
3. for which the company is capable of developing a better solution than the benchmark for that area.

It is even possible to measure the degree of improvement required and hence the proportion of the development effort that should be put into achieving this. This is done by:

- using the user ratings of performance given to each existing solution (including your own candidate or existing product) to each sought benefit;

- determining a target performance level based on the elements of the marketing objectives, product strategy and distinctive competencies of the company;

- weighting this by the relative importance of each factor.

Aspects of the product that have been targeted in this way for superior performance over the competition's, become the main sales points, or to use advertising terminology, the product's proposition USP (unique selling). During subsequent marketing, they allow you to distinguish the product in ways that customers value and that make best use of the company's abilities.

It is arguable that such measures really only apply to incremental developments of essentially similar solutions to existing problems. Even then care must be taken, because relative performance is often not linear, with an inordinate amount of effort being required to produce an improvement so small in the users' eyes that it is not cost effective to provide it. This is another area where the techniques of feature/benefit optimisation (described later) can help.

The wider application of QFD

So far we have concentrated on examining the ways in which QFD can assist in the process of product definition, but its usefulness does not stop there. The QFD chart can actually be expanded to any level of detail you like. At first it may examine only the top level attributes of a product described in broad terms. When you are examining a particular facet of a product the process outlined earlier can also be used to expand the relevant attributes, examining the precise relationship between customer quality and the minute details of the product that provides it.

For example, in the alarm clock examined earlier, consideration may move on to the detail of the time display. The quality characteristics may then be expanded to include the design, size, aspect ratio and colour of the characters used, the colour of the background, the reflectivity of both etc. Most (if not all) of these physical attributes of the product can be measured and investigations carried out to determine how customer acceptance relates to the physical measure (this should be done using existing products as part of the experiments to provide a 'real world' reference). If this is carried through to its logical conclusion, the QFD chart can ultimately be used:

- during product definition, to determine what elements should be developed;

- during design and implementation, as a basis for measuring how well the development is achieving its goals;

- in production, to provide quantified quality targets. (For further details of this, refer to the book *Quality Function Deployment*.)

QFD in context

The process of applying QFD during product definition outlined in these pages may seem daunting, particularly to those new to the technique who have not yet developed their own approach to it and systems for applying it. The alternative, which is widely practised, is to develop the product you think is right based on your experience, saving all this effort and spending the resources on actual product development instead. If the product is very simple (eg satisfies a single, non-complex customer need with a single, non-complex product function), this may well be a perfectly valid method. However, very many products are complex and, to be successful, must satisfy needs in ways that distinguish them from the competition. The thinking process inherent in QFD guides the team to better solutions in these more complex cases.

Neither should applying QFD be such a burden. When it is first adopted by a company it will undoubtedly take some time to collect verbatims and build and analyse the chart. A great deal of this time can be saved on subsequent occasions if:

- the team can refine the technique to suit your company circumstances;

- the team can help transfer the skills to new teams;
- information gathering can be made a natural part of the customer interface;
- once gathered, verbatims need only be monitored for subsequent occasions—there should normally be no need to start from scratch each time.

CONCEPT DEVELOPMENT

We have discussed a rational process of defining the development objectives as a seven stage process. The first three of these stages have so far been examined:

1. Setting corporate goals and constraints.
2. Understanding the market and the customer; defining what constitutes the 'total product'.
3. Using QFD to determine what aspects of the product produce customer satisfaction (or delight).

The next step, referred to here as *concept development*, develops potential solutions to these now well understood customer needs. In the search for a more effective and logical process of product development, no pretence should be made that every aspect can be laid down as a universal procedure. This stage of concept development is not put forward, therefore, as a process in its own right, but as part of the overall method which teams must carry out using their own skill, ingenuity and experience.

It is most important that potential solutions to customer wants (or needs) are developed that form part of the company's overall strategy and can be effectively exploited. Furthermore, any such solutions offered by the development team must be shown to produce value to the customer. We will examine how this can be measured in the next section.

It is not suggested, however, that there must be no product development until this stage; the absolute requirement for bringing products to market rapidly would make this unacceptable in most cases. A good approach is for a mental model of the product to be created, perhaps by one person (the product champion). This can take place very early in the process described so far, before any systematic study of the market takes place. Depending on how new to the company the product is, technical feasibility together with more or less tangible product development may take place early, both to reduce time-to-market and to reduce technical risk. If the product and its associated technology (including manufacturing technology) *are* relatively new, it will be essential for this level of development to take place whilst market investigation and QFD are being carried out in parallel. More will be said on the subject of parallel development and risk reduction in Chapter 3.

Up to this point any such development should be regarded as the *prototyping* of ideas, not the development of the real product. If such work is regarded as real product development, a high degree of resistance to discarding—even modifying—it will occur, either within the team or by those who might argue not to 'waste' the work already done. This is a dangerous situation for two reasons. First, the standard of the work that is put into prototyping can be much lower (because the prototype is produced much faster). Secondly it makes people resistant to developing new ideas, ie complete solutions to the whole product rather than piecemeal demonstrations of parts of the product.

Concept development, therefore, is required to capitalise on the new knowledge gained from QFD. It explores how the sought benefits can be provided using the skills and resources available to the company. In many areas of a product this process may produce only one logical solution; in others there may be several solutions. Which should be developed? Should the development proceed at all? These are questions which must be addressed before too much resource is expended.

To reduce the risk of wasting resources, this stage should only take the development as far as:

1. listing potential solutions to the sought benefits;
2. determining that they can indeed be developed with the resources available (at least with a sufficiently high degree of confidence);
3. exploring the solutions sufficiently to understand all of the implications to the customer and the interactions between different parts of the product;
4. producing stimulus material to test the acceptability of these solutions. Such materials may include technical proofs of principle, but should also include models to test market acceptability.

DETERMINING CUSTOMER VALUE

The team may now be faced with options about how the product should look and how it can carry out some of its functions. In some cases these different options will appeal to different segments of the market (as may have been determined earlier). If these are individually viable and jointly cover the original marketing objectives, all that remains is to test their market acceptability and to fully develop the product (see page 78).

The decisions facing the team are often more complex than this. What should the team do if two or more of the demanded benefits are in conflict? What if the whole product costs too much? What if the total market for the product is so fragmented into differing segments, that none are individually viable? The answer is to try to measure the *relative value* buyers will place on these options (or elements of the product), and use these values to optimise the product specification—to maximise overall market share or margin or some combination of both.

No measurement of these relative values can ever be perfectly accurate for many reasons, including the fact that all customers are different, and measuring more than a small sample will be very expensive. Furthermore, any measurement at this stage can be no more than a prediction of how they may react when faced with real buying decisions. What is needed at this stage are measures to reduce certain risks:

- that the product fails to meet the requirements of a large enough proportion of potential customers;

- that the need for several products is overlooked;

- that the product fails to generate as much value as it is capable of in the customers' eyes.

To achieve these things, the team needs to know:

1. The worth that potential customers place on individual features in the product (where these features are optional). Given that there will rarely be a one-to-one mapping between sought benefit and product feature, this is in effect the relative worth customers will (sub-consciously) use when making trade-off decisions between options.
2. The relative importance of different elements of the total product, *including price.*
3. Differences between groups of potential customers in these measures.

The technique that has been developed to provide this information is called *conjoint analysis* (or *preference research*). Put simply, it asks potential customers their preferences between several alternative products, and from this information infers their attitudes towards individual elements within a product. The difficulty with the technique is that of obtaining realistic results.

The following steps provide a general guide to this technique as used in the development of tangible products where the customer might be expected to exert choice during purchasing. Earlier research into the market should have established whether customers actually shop for products in this way. Other forms of customer buying behaviour might indicate that the value of conjoint analysis is limited. This may be true of impulse purchases (although research, including conjoint research, should establish this by showing, for example, that instant appeal to the senses or on an emotional level is far more important that any other aspect of the product).

What to test

The first step is to determine what elements of a product are optional and which of the options need to be tested. The QFD information should be the starting point for this. Aspects that probably need to be tested will:

- map onto several sought benefits where the linkages are both positive and negative (ie it provides one benefit but detracts from another);

- map onto benefits where there is evidence that customer attitudes are not homogenous (ie customers vary significantly in their relative rating of the benefits);

- have more than one physical solution, particularly where the differences between them are significant in
  —performance
  —looks
  —development or product cost
  —time-to-market.

In the case of the last two, they are only worth testing if the outcome will be perceived to be different by the customers. Tests should therefore be made whenever a clear case for a single solution can't be made. These considerations apply to all elements of the *total product*, not just physical features. It is perfectly possible to measure the value placed on, for example, extended warrantees.

How to test it

There are many ways in which conjoint analysis can be carried out, but most revolve around two techniques—*pairwise comparisons* and *full profile testing*. In pairwise comparisons respondents are asked to make trade-off decisions between only one pair of features of a product at a time, eg processor speed vs. price for a computer. In this example, if there are potentially three price points and three processor speeds, nine options are produced which the respondent must put into order of preference. By the time several different features are compared, respondent fatigue can be a problem. The pairwise technique is also criticised for being extremely artificial. In reality the customer will be faced with choices between complete products, not just a pair of features. The full profile technique capitalises on this: it presents respondents with choices between complete products which vary in a controlled way. Although the pairwise technique can have its uses, particularly if administered using computer aided techniques, this discussion will be restricted to the full profile version of conjoint analysis.

The next consideration is the number of different elements of the product that need to be tested, together with the number of options that exist within each element. Using the example of alarm clocks, the elements and options that could be tested might include:

Element	*Options*
display type:	analogue, digital, projection (onto ceiling)
illumination switched on:	permanent, on demand (manual), automatic (senses low light levels)
method of switching alarm off:	manual, sound switch, proximity sensor
price:	£14.99, £19.99, £24.99

In the jargon of conjoint analysis, each element of the product that is to be varied is called a *factor*. Each option is called a *level* for that factor.

To ask potential customers their preferences amongst all possible factors and levels would be a massive task, as there are 81 different complete products ($3\times3\times3\times3$ options) just from these four features. Fortunately statistical techniques have been developed that allow a smaller number of combinations to be used to measure customer attitudes to individual features. With this information it is possible to simulate what their preferences would be to the complete set, and thence to work out the most preferred option.

The technique involves constructing an *orthogonal array*, where the presence of any individual level within one factor is not linked to the presence of any other option. Together with statistical techniques, this permits the measurement of the relative worths that respondents are placing on individual options, as each is independent of all others. In this way the potential 81 complete products in the above example can be reduced to 9, a manageable number for testing.

The construction of these orthogonal arrays is not particularly simple. A small number of software packages exist which generate them automatically from lists of factors and levels. Alternatively, standard array designs can be adapted from the literature.*

A potential problem with this reduction should be borne in mind. Such a dramatic reduction in the number of complete options presented for ranking only allows the measurement of the relative worth of each feature as present individually (called *main effects*); it is incapable of measuring effects where the presence of one option affects the relative worth of a different feature. For example, a permanently illuminated analogue display may be considered more acceptable to some than a permanently illuminated digital display. These so-called *second order effects* must be considered when designing the research. If it is believed that such effects may happen, larger experiments must be used to test more of the options in combination.

Another consideration is what to do about technically difficult (or even impossible) combinations of features. For example, it might be technically very difficult to provide a projection display (where the time can be read on the ceiling or wall) that is permanently illuminated. In these circumstances there is a temptation to eliminate difficult combinations from the research. However, if this is done, the array is no longer orthogonal and reliable analysis becomes impossible. The options open in these circumstances are, firstly, to leave things as they are, complete with difficult combinations. If the implausibility of the combinations will be obvious to respondents, then the second option is to construct a hybrid product element from the two elements, where only valid combinations are present. This option is not preferred as you will never discover what value might be placed on certain combinations. If this were sufficiently high, it might outweigh the difficulty of producing it.

If there are a large number of alternatives that must be tested, and especially when there are several factors which must be represented with a large number of levels, even the minimum size orthogonal array can become too large to expect respondents to be able to rank them all. Depending on who the respondents are and how well they are motivated to spend sufficient time ranking alternatives, this might be the case with as few as 15–20 alternatives. Indeed, it could be argued that the test ceases to be at all representative of real purchase choice if the options get too numerous. If this occurs, there are several choices available:

- Reduce the maximum number of levels or the number of factors. This is particularly relevant when the levels represent a contin-

---

*Addelman, Sidney (1962) *Orthogonal Main-Effect Plans for Asymmetrical Factorial Experiments*, Technometrics, 4, Feb pp 21–46.

uum, as with price. These can often be limited to a small number without reducing the amount of *useful* data gathered.

* Split the test up. Different factors could be explored in different experiments, taking great care that common factors and levels exist to allow inter-experiment comparison (price would normally be used) and that differences between groups of respondents are not significant.

* Use computer-aided interviewing. Software packages exist* that allow more extensive testing using combinations of
  —self-ranking of features, where features deemed to be unimportant by each respondent can be eliminated from further testing;
  —pairwise comparisons using limited sets of options; and
  —full profile comparisons, either by comparing full profile alternatives in pairs or by ranking lists as described above.

Preparing the stimulus

Having chosen which factors to test and what the levels need to be for each factor, we now need to make the comparisons as realistic as possible. How this is achieved will depend a great deal on who the subjects for research are, and what familiarity they have with the products being tested. As a general rule, the less familiar they are, the more realistic the stimulus must be.

This becomes obvious if you consider investigating the acceptability of a completely new feature, or a new technical solution to a user need that will have unfamiliar performance (or other) implications. For example, alarm clocks now exist where the alarm can be switched off simply by waving a hand near the clock (referred to earlier as a 'proximity sensor'). Existing technology uses an infra-red detector that has a fan shaped sensing area. Because of its power consumption, it can only be used to switch the alarm off in a non-mains powered clock; it could not be left on all the time in order to be used, for example, to illuminate the time display. Supposing you wanted to test the acceptability of a new sensor, with a more evenly shaped sensing area, lower power consumption (so it can be used as a light switch at all times), but with a slightly smaller sensing range. It is highly unlikely that you will find any potential respondents who will understand the implications of these differences, so in this case some practical demonstration will need to be arranged prior to the conjoint experiment.

Another technique is to use mock advertisements as stimulus. In this case you need to consider very carefully how you will communi-

---

*For example, the *ACA System*, Sawtooth Software, Evanston, USA.

cate any features that are not already familiar to respondents, and then design mocked-up adverts or pack designs to get the benefits across. To be fair, similar stimulus must be used for the other features. Ultimately this could lead to complete advert (or pack) mock-ups being used for each alternative in the conjoint experiment. More cost effectively however, the stimulus would be used to familiarise respondents with the individual product features prior to the actual ranking of alternatives.

The research

Given that it is impossible (in most markets) to research all potential customers, and that customer attitudes will vary across the population, recruiting *representative* research subjects is crucial. Earlier research into the market and the results of gathering statements of sought benefit will have resulted in a wealth of information about who these customers are and how they might vary in their attitudes to the benefits they seek. This should form the basis for recruiting representative cross sections for conjoint analysis.

Ideally you would recruit respondents who are just on the point of purchasing such products. If this is a regularly bought item, this may be perfectly feasible. However, many products are purchased infrequently, and unless the recruits are on the verge of buying, they may not be sufficiently familiar with the product class in general to be at all useful to your research. In these circumstances it may be more acceptable to recruit existing owners than to pay the—potentially very high—recruitment costs involved in finding respondents at the exact point of buying. In some product classes (especially with professional and industrial products) the buying decision process can be very protracted, in which case finding informed potential customers (rather than existing owners) may be much simpler.

The conduct of the research will have to be tailored to your needs. If small numbers are sufficient and if significant familiarisation is needed, then preference research may be added to focus groups. For larger numbers, and especially when only limited familiarisation is required, hall tests could provide a suitable vehicle.

During the research, respondents will be asked to place a number of alternative products in order of preference (or to score each of them, with 100 = their ideal product). A common technique is to give them a set of cards, each one describing a version of the complete product in words (possibly even with pictures to make things clearer). Their responses must be recorded, along with other details that might allow you to link different types of response to criteria that could be used during later marketing of the product. For example, if you find that there are significant differences in the worth that respondents place on certain features, and these differences are linked to, say, age or sex, this will be invaluable when targeting marketing communications post-launch. Opportunities to gather this data should not be overlooked, but do not overload respondents by asking them for too much information!

Table 2.2 Example options for an alarm clock

Results from a single respondent

Display type	Illumination	Alarm switch-off	Price (£)	Ranking
analogue	automatic	proximity	24.99	6
digital	manual	manual	24.99	12
digital	automatic	sound	14.99	3
analogue	manual	sound	19.99	11
projection	manual	proximity	14.99	9
analogue	permanent	manual	14.99	4
projection	automatic	manual	19.99	5
projection	permanent	sound	24.99	8
digital	permanent	proximity	19.99	2
analogue	permanent	proximity	14.99	1
analogue	manual	proximity	19.99	10
digital	automatic	sound	24.99	7

NB there are 12 alternatives listed above due to the inclusion of 3 *hold-outs* as explained later.

Analysis

Assuming all the features present in the experiment are truly orthogonal, analysis is relatively straightforward. Each product will have been assigned its rank order-of-preference number (or rating number out of, say, 100) and these will be determined by the utility values (called *part-worths* in the jargon) respondents place on each individual feature. Multiple regression analysis (provided with most sophisticated spread-sheet packages these days) will yield these part-worths. Specialised software packages also exist* which speed the calculations required and will also provide the re-scaling necessary and the calculation of the *relative importance* of each factor. This measures the relative spread in the part-worths of each level of each factor, and provides a useful measure of how important

---

*Both the SPSS and the *Aca System* (see notes on pp 57 and 66) provide this.

each aspect of the whole product is. Within each factor, the part-worths measure the 'value' respondents place on each of the options (or features). If these features include price, we now have the raw information we require to optimise the product specification. Mathematically, this is represented as:

Rank order for product A = Sum of (part worths of each factor level present) + Constant

For example, the above conjoint experiment gives the results shown in Table 2.3 for a single respondent (NB the test would normally be carried out on a number of respondents).

Table 2.3 Relative importance of product features

Factor	Level	Part-worth	Relative importance
Display	analogue digital projection	÷0.3 1.0 ÷0.7	13
Illumination	permanent manual automatic	2.0 ÷4.0 2.0	47
Alarm switch	manual sound proximity	÷0.3 ÷0.7 1.0	13
Price (£)	14.99 19.99 24.99	1.3 0.7 ÷2.0	13

This shows that for this particular respondent, the method of illumination is most important, with other elements having equal weight. He or she has normal pricing expectations, ie has placed a higher intrinsic value on cheaper products, although not in a linear fashion (the last £5 increase produces twice the impact of the first). The ideal clock in this instance would be digital, automatic or permanently illuminated (the respondent does not distinguish between them) with a proximity switch for the alarm, costing £14.99. If this combination is not possible (eg the price point may be too low to be able to incorporate these features), the next section will discuss how the product can be specified for optimum results.

Before moving on to product optimisation, we need to consider

statistics once more. We have already considered the need to
ensure that the sample of respondents is representative. The other
issues are:

1. how reliable each response is;
2. how important a particular feature across the whole potential
    market is.

Reliability of response can be measured to a certain extent by the
inclusion of *hold-out cards*. These are full profile products, representing options as with all the other alternatives, but they are in
excess of the minimum number required for an orthogonal array,
and—most importantly—they are not used in the calculation of part-
worths. They can therefore be used to test the reliability of the
response, by calculating the total utility, relating this to rank order
(or preference score) and comparing this result with how it was
actually ranked by the respondent. Responses with a poor measure
of reliability calculated in this way can be discarded.

In the above example, the hold-out cards have calculated ranks of
2, 10 and 7, compared to their actual ranks of 1, 10 and 7. This indicates a good degree of reliability from this respondent. As explained
earlier, deviation from the predicted order could be caused by second
order effects, which can't be determined with this experimental
design.

Point two above refers again to the issue of population variation
and segmentation. If all respondents produce the same or similar
part-worths, then you have a homogenous population and some
fairly easy decisions to make about product optimisation. If, as often
happens, clusters appear (where different factors are important to
different groups), the optimisation process is more difficult, but still
possible. There is a growing trend amongst customer focused
companies to cater for the *varying* needs of their markets, something that can only be done if:

* the individual groups of customers are large enough to make the
  differentiated product viable;

* the company is capable of developing such products highly efficiently;

* product range and architecture are chosen with the needs of a
  highly differentiated market firmly in mind (eg commonality of
  parts);

* techniques such as these are used effectively to segment the
  market by product.

FEATURE/BENEFIT OPTIMISATION

We have now gathered nearly all the information we need to optimise the value generated by the product. In this case, the word *optimise* refers to a choice between these options (depending on the strategic goals defined earlier):

- At one extreme, producing the largest *margin* (the difference between the cost to produce the product and its average nett selling price).

- At the other, producing the largest possible *volume of sales* (by gaining a large share of the existing market, or through expanding the market). This would be expected to produce the largest long-term profits (see Porter, page 29).

- In between, trading off margin for volume to maximise the product of *margin* times *volume*. This produces the largest contribution to overall company profitability from the product, and might normally be the preferred aim.

Cost

By now we have gathered all the information we need to determine what aspects of the product generate value (and, as we will see later, potential volume); what is missing is the cost side of the equation. There are two essential elements of this:

1. cost of goods (may also be called 'factory gate price'); and
2. amortised development and tooling costs.

Both of these are volume dependent (although the latter may be more directly so), and the approach suggested in this section is not simplistic—these volume dependencies must be estimated and taken into account. Individual company policy on development cost amortisation must also be taken into account—if one doesn't exist it must be created. In reality, development costs will vary depending on which product options are eventually chosen. In practice it may be too difficult to estimate these differences particularly accurately, so some baseline development cost may be chosen until the final specification can be defined.

Product cost

From the above, the cost of goods is the first cost element we must concern ourselves with when optimising the product. In a truly integrated team, technical and manufacturing specialists will have been involved early on in the project. Apart from their very valuable inputs to QFD and to assessing feasibility, one of their early roles will be to develop a costing model. This allows the team to calculate the cost of design options rapidly, and for this purpose accuracy may be sacrificed for usability and speed. A common complaint at this stage is that many components (particularly those manufactured by other parties) may not be costed rationally by the manufacturer. This may be so, but it should not prevent a well balanced and experienced team from developing estimating procedures. Whilst individual suppliers may not cost rationally, provided supply is competitive, prices must ultimately be based on rational variables such as those listed below.

The costing model is likely to be based on parameters that are simple to estimate, such as component counts, breakdown of labour and machine operations, material volumes and process timings and so on. Any such estimates should be tested for accuracy by obtaining proper quotes. The same is obviously true of the overall costing model—tests for accuracy must be made at various stages, depending on the team's assessment of the risks involved.

A problem frequently encountered with developing costing models at this stage is the need to retain confidentiality, often exacerbated by the fact that many suppliers seem to have difficulties costing new products. One technique that usefully overcomes this is to select a 'shadow' product. This involves choosing a currently available product that is similar in components, materials, production methods, volume and price to the envisaged new product. This can then be used to gain a detailed understanding of the costs without disclosing confidential details. It has the added advantage of allowing you to source potential suppliers on the basis of applicable experience. To develop this model the team will need to gather in data on a number of factors:

- component prices (and volume breaks);

- material costs;

- process costs;

- labour; activity times and hourly rates;

- factory mark-up structure for overheads and profit (how they are attributed to individual direct cost elements);

- transport costs;

- duty and exchange rates as applicable;

- component distribution channel mark-up structure.

All of the above data can be gathered in parallel with the product definition process described so far, although some details may not be complete until the 'concept development' stage. In some industries (notably personal computing at present), these costs are fluid, and projections must be made to the likely costs at time of launch and beyond.

From this data it should be possible to construct a mathematical model, using spreadsheet software (or pencil and paper!), that will allow the rapid costing of alternative product options and configurations.

Development cost

Although cost of goods is often the largest and apparently most important contributor to product cost, it is worth adding a few words of warning about pursuing the goal of lower product cost too far. For any given set of features there will be an optimum amount of development to achieve lowest product cost. Figure 2.2 illustrates this.

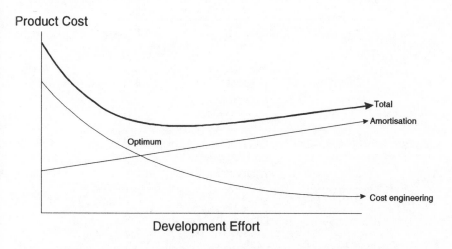

Figure 2.2 Development cost affects product cost

There will be a certain amount of development that will enable the set of features to be achieved at all. Beyond that level of development, simple cost engineering measures can have a dramatic effect on the cost of goods. However, a law of diminishing returns begins to apply at some point, and more effort produces ever smaller reductions in the cost of goods. At the same time, all this extra development effort has to be recovered, either by amortising the costs by increasing the total product cost (as illustrated) or by a reduction in gross margin. No matter how it is looked at, development costs *must* be paid for, and there is thus an optimum amount of effort worth applying.

Trading-off cost and value

Everything is now finally in place to make decisions about the specification of the product. We know what produces value, and how the market varies in this respect. We know how the costs of potential products build up and how this is volume dependent. It should now be a straightforward matter to determine the margins generated by various product feature combinations.

Normally the starting point is to look at an existing product or, failing that, some minimum specification product. Let us say that in the example in table 2.4, the product (clock) has an analogue display and is switched off and illuminated with manual switches. As this is the lowest cost set of options, let us assume that it matches the lowest retail price point researched.

Table 2.4 Product specifications *vs.* worth (value)

Factor	Level	Part-worth
Display	analogue	÷0.3
	digital	1.0
	projection	÷0.7
	permanent	2.0
Illumination	manual	÷4.0
	automatic	2.0
	manual	÷0.3
Alarm switch	sound	÷0.7
	proximity	1.0
	14.99	1.3
Price (£)	19.99	0.7
	24.99	÷2.0

The next step is to cost this product and calculate the margin. In our example, let us assume that our ex-factory prices are one third of retail, ie this £15.00 clock will bring us a nett average sales value of £5.00. If all the features above cost £4.00 (cost of goods plus amortised investment), the margin is £1.00 or 20 per cent. (NB In this example, costs are chosen to illustrate the point rather than for realism.)

This provides the baseline against which other combinations can be assessed. It should now be possible to improve the margin by varying the combination of features used. Starting with features that have little or no difference in part worth (eg replacing the manual alarm switch with a sound activated one), which yields the lowest overall product cost? If there is no other evidence to contradict this choice from QFD and all the other market research, this is the better solution.

When it comes to trade-offs between features where the part-worths vary, the task is to assess in monetary terms the difference in customer value they generate. If the difference in part-worths is within the range associated with different price points, this is a reasonable approximation. For example the part-worth of adding a proximity switch over a manual switch is 1.3. This is equivalent to the change in part-worth associated with a change in retail price from £15 to something between £20 and £25. To retain equivalent customer value the product could be around 50 per cent more expensive, producing an ex-works sales value of £7.50.

If the total cost of adding a feature (not forgetting to amortise investment!) produces a higher margin from the potentially higher sales price, it is better to add it. In this case, if we assume that the nett incremental cost of adding proximity sensing is £1.50, the margin would be 27 per cent ((7.5–5.5)/7.5). This is higher than our baseline margin, so we should add the feature.

The problem with this rather simplistic method is that it can only be used when changes in part-worths between feature trade-offs fall within the range of part-worths generated at the different price points researched. If this is not the case, it is not reasonable to extrapolate outside these price points. It also assumes that the values generated by adding more than one new feature are additive. This is a limitation of conjoint plans which explore main effects only.

The technique also uses only a summary of the data gathered earlier, and, although simple, fails to make best use of the information available.

Share of preference

A more subtle and powerful technique than the simple optimis-ation discussed above is to forecast market share for various com-binations of features, including price. Although this sounds daunting, it is actually a fairly simple task utilising the information gathered during QFD and conjoint research.

The first step is to build a model of the market. If you believe that the sample of respondents used for the above research is represent-ative of the whole market, this model consists of the database of part-worths each respondent places on the researched features. This may be expanded to include features not directly researched by using the QFD results to pro-rate the importance of other aspects of a product.

The model may also be expanded or modified by using *synthetic data*, rather than the raw data from research. This synthetic data would be generated from the research results, with records to represent the behaviour of each cluster within the market. The advantage of using synthetic data is that it allows the team to take into account other factors not adequately represented in the research results. When generating such synthetic data you are likely to come across linkages to product attributes that you don't have data on. For example, you may have preference research results on display, switch and price, and have market share data on portable vs. bedside product format available separately, but how do individual purchasers link (say) portability and display type? The choice of optimum product range could crucially depend on whether one (researched) feature is linked to another (even if researched by other means). Experimenting with different versions of a synthetic model will allow you to uncover these sensitivities. If they exist, you will need to gather data on the linkages between them.

The danger is that such a model may become too divorced from the raw data that it is meant to represent. As long as this danger is recognised, checks can be made to test for variations between the synthetic results and those from the original data, taking into account deliberate modifications or simplifications.

The relative preference score of real and potential products can now be calculated for each respondent (or cluster). In each session, groups of competing products can be assessed, where a 'sale' is recorded for the product that produces the highest preference score for an individual member of the population. The proportion of 'sales' for each product represents potential market share (assuming all are marketed equally effectively!). For example, Table 2.5 illustrates reducing the number of features for the sake of clarity. In this case products A, B and C are the existing main competitors and product D is the first of the potential products to be experimented with. This option gains 35 per cent of the preference market by being the first choice of segments 3 and 4. The contribution (margin times sales volume) for this can now be calculated and compared with that generated by other options.

To add greater refinement to a summarised model, it can be expanded to include measures of the distribution on each factor for each segment. Monte Carlo simulation will then allow measures of the possible variance in market share. This will provide a useful input into a formal assessment of marketing risk, as discussed in

Table 2.5 Share of preference market

seg.	no.	Factors									Candidate or competing products				sale
		Display			Switch			Price			Prod A	Prod B	Prod C	Prod D	
		A	B	C	a	b	c	x	y	z	Aax	Bcz	Abz	Ccz	
1	40	-0.3	1.0	-0.7	-0.3	-0.7	1.0	1.3	0.7	-2.0	0.7	1.3	-3.0	-1.7	B
2	25	1.5	-1.0	-0.5	1.0	-0.5	-0.5	2.0	0	-2.0	4.5	-3.5	-1.0	-3.0	A
3	25	-2.0	0.8	1.2	-1.7	1.0	0.7	1.0	0.5	-1.5	-2.7	0	-2.5	0.2	D
4	10	-1.4	0.2	1.2	-3.0	1.0	2.0	0.5	0.3	-0.8	-3.9	1.4	-1.2	2.4	D

Chapter 3. The model of customer preference can ultimately be used in several ways:

- To test the potential market share of a proposed concept against existing products (as described above).

- To refine the product, experimenting with alternative features to gain a greater share of preference.

- To assess the need for a range of products, possibly based around a common core with options to suit different clusters.

- To test the impact of competitors improving their products in response to your launch.

- To test the impact of a new product (either yours or a competitor's) on the market share of your existing products if they compete in the same markets.

PRODUCT DEVELOPMENT

The product (or products if the need for more than one has been identified) can now be developed. The product definition process described in these pages will have achieved:

- A clear understanding of the corporate reasons for developing this product. Potentially, this will allow measures to be used so that the team can be rewarded for the success they bring to the company.

- Deeper insights into the marketing issues surrounding the product; who the customers are, what they want, how to communicate with them, what important sales messages must be vindicated by the product.

- Knowledge of what constitutes 'the total product', including elements of the augmented product often ignored until the development is complete.

- An understanding of how to produce customer satisfaction; what benefits customers seek and (in detail) how physical attributes of the product relate to them.

- How to measure the value customers will place on the options you are capable of developing for them.

- How these options affect the cost of the product.

- How to specify a product that will produce the greatest returns.

All that remains now is to get on with it! The following chapters deal with the main management issues involved during such developments, with particular emphasis on the team approach that is central to integrated product development.

Applicability

At the beginning of chapter 1 we discussed briefly the fact that this highly rational process of product definition does not necessarily apply to all products. Specifically we excluded commodity items that are distinguished mainly by price, branding and other non-product elements of the marketing mix. Does the process therefore apply to all other types of product? Superficially it could be argued that it only applies where the purchasing decision is made rationally with free comparisons made between competing products.

It is worth examining the way in which products are classified by buyer attitude to see if this argument is valid. There are four standard classifications:*

1. **Convenience products** are bought frequently, immediately and with the minimum of effort in comparison and buying (eg consumables such as paper and tobacco products). Product availability and immediate appeal to the senses are likely to be more important than product features.
2. **Shopping products** are products that the customer, in the process of selection and purchase, characteristically compares on such bases as suitability, quality, price and design. The product definition process is ideally suited to this category.
3. **Speciality products** have unique characteristics and/or brand identification for which a significant group of buyers are habitually willing to make a special purchasing effort (eg specialist cars and hi-fi products). In this case it is vital that the providers understand the special requirements of their niche market. Arguably the process described here should be easier to apply as the market is easy to reach and may be more willing to participate in research that produces products better tailored to *their* needs.
4. **Unsought products** are ones that the customer does not know about or knows about but does not normally think of buying. Many new products fall into this category until effective marketing communications and significant market penetration make the customer aware of them, for example smoke detectors and

---

*Kotler (1988) *Marketing Management: Analysis, Planning, Implementation and Control*, Prentice Hall International Inc, New Jersey. Kotler applies this classification to consumer products, but it is equally applicable to those bought by industry and professionals.

video cassette recorders. The definition process is important in this class too, because although they may not be compared with others at first, better products that are more likely to succeed in the long term will result **if** they are well matched to the customers' requirements. There is a real danger with developing any new product in this category based on an isolated perception of the customer's needs—the risk of that perception being wrong is too great, given the cost of developing most products these days. It may be more difficult to apply some of the techniques outlined in these pages, but the need to get it right is arguably greater.

In conclusion, most products compete by satisfying their purchasers' needs better than any alternatives. Even if the purchasing decision is not entirely rational and based on fair comparisons between products, greater success will still come from some combination of:

- lower returns rates due to 'product unsuitable';

- improved customer perception of overall quality;

- improved repeat purchase;

- more frequent recommendation;

- more retailers or dealers wanting to carry the product.

This product definition process is therefore recommended as a means of lowering the risk of market failure *and* improving the speed of getting to market by cutting through the vague and slow process used by most companies.

3

Risk in NPD

Product development is a risky business, and most companies can recall horror stories of developments that produced the wrong product, produced it too late, cost far too much and resulted in a ridiculously expensive product or one which customers failed to buy. None of these risks should, however, be accepted simply as a natural part of new developments. Indeed, the whole purpose of this book is to show that risk, in all its forms, *can* be reduced to acceptable levels during NPD.

Elsewhere we discuss at length the measures to reduce certain forms of risk:

- that the product doesn't fulfil the company's objectives or takes it in the wrong direction;

- that the product fails to meet customer requirements and can't be communicated or distributed and sold effectively;

- that the product fails to generate value for the company (ie it costs too much, is worth too little or sales volumes will be too low);

- that the wrong people are brought together to develop the product;

- that the team can't work together effectively or take too long to do so;

- that the team don't understand what they need to achieve in order to produce success for the company through the product.

Before discussing individual sources of risk and specific actions that can be taken, it is worth looking at risk as an element of product development to be managed in its own right.

RISK MANAGEMENT

Here we introduce the subject of risk in product development and suggest a thinking framework for managing it. It is by no means an exhaustive coverage of a very complex subject.

Under many circumstances there are some highly refined

numeric techniques available for assessing risk (eg FMEA—Failure Modes Effects Analysis). These can be very difficult to use during technical product development as they rely on statistical or probabilistic techniques that require quantified information rarely available during NPD.

One lesson worth taking from these techniques is the fact that every risk has an associated *probability* and *severity*. Before deciding what management action to take, it is vital to stop and consider, first, how likely is this to occur? and secondly, what are the consequences if it does happen? (immediate costs plus knock-on effects etc.).

The structure of risk

There is a danger that because risk involves the unknown, it somehow defies rational thought. This must be avoided in order to allow positive risk management steps to be taken and to allow risk to be high on the management agenda. Risk can in fact be thought to have a structure of its own, one that involves some or all of the following elements.

Sources: Weakness

Internal or intrinsic sources of risk can be seen as weaknesses that to a greater or lesser extent can be overcome. They might include:

- Ignorance
- Human error
- Lack of resources
- Lack of experience
- Lack of training
- Failure of teams to work together effectively
- Unknown or unproven technology.

Threats

Coming from the outside, these sources of risk are much harder to predict. They include:

- Supplier activity (failure, change of specification etc.)
- Competitor activity (pre-emptive product launch, price war etc.)
- Customer behaviour (demand changes, changes in perception etc.)

- Political change (eg legislation affecting your products or customers)
- Natural forces.

Modifying factors

No risk should just be accepted as it is: all of these basic sources of risk are susceptible to modification to decrease their severity. This chapter suggests some methods for their modification.

Consequences

Most of these are obvious and reflect the three dimensions of project achievement:

- Time over-runs
- Development cost over-runs
- Product cost too high
- Non-achievement of technical goals
- Non-achievement of commercial goals
- Knock-on effects on other projects
- Impact on rest of company.

Sources of risk

More helpful than categorising risk as simply internal or external is to identify the two generic sources—market risk and technical risk.

Technical risk is the risk of failing to hit the target—in one of the three dimensions:

1. Failure to meet specification—a function that cannot be provided, an incorrect size, a poor quality level etc. (the 'achievement' dimension of the project goal).
2. Failure to deliver the product within the time frame required for maximum product success—eg missing a public show for launch (the time dimension).
3. Failing in the expenditure dimension, ie delivering a product that costs too much to produce or has cost too much to develop and bring to market.

Marketing risk is really failure caused by specifying the wrong target. There are a multitude of ways in which this could occur, eg:

- Failing to identify a market which is large enough or profitable enough (through adding value) to warrant the development.

- Failing to understand customer requirements within the chosen market and to forecast how these might change.

- Failing to anticipate competitor activity.

- Failing to forecast changes within the market (growth, usage patterns, new solutions to needs etc.)

- Failing to allow for macro-economic changes (tax regimes, recession etc.)

- Failing to forecast the product market life cycle (rate of uptake, market share, timing).

Augmented risk could be classed as a third source—caused by the joint action of marketing and technical risks. One of the common market risk avoidance techniques is to over-specify the product, for example to provide a high level of features in order to 'be sure of' satisfying user requirements and to make life difficult for competitors. The problem with this is that over-specifying features (or specifying an earlier than necessary launch date or unrealistically low cost) will almost certainly cause the technical development team more difficulties, which will in turn increase the risk of being late, causing the cost to escalate or some of the performance requirements to be missed or omitted. Thus one source of risk has been amplified by the action of the other, creating a vicious circle.

Planning for risk

The following stages provide a framework for managing risk.

Recognise

The first step is to identify as many of the possible sources of risk as you can, as early as you can. Make this a deliberate part of the planning process by involving people with other skills and experience. Hold a brain-storming session to list and evaluate potential sources of risk. Consider carefully the make-up of the team needed for this. In addition to making sure all the right disciplines are included, consider the natural team roles (see Chapter 4) of those available to make this session as effective as possible. Often there is at least one person in every company with a reputation of being a 'Jonah'—particularly good at spotting what might go wrong: make sure such a person is included if at all possible.

Many of these risks can just be accepted, or managed in a non-specific way such as through training, increasing the available resource or making justifiable allowances in your estimates of time scale and cost.

Avoid

Some risks can simply be side-stepped. In many cases there are alternative development routes that can just step around a potential source of risk, provided you know what you are avoiding. If this is not possible, consider how the risk potential could be shared with others, by bringing new expertise or experience to bear on the problem.

Consider also how the risk could be transferred to others: specialists who may be prepared to solve the problem for you for a fixed commitment on your part. This could include suppliers who may be prepared to modify their specifications or contract terms to help you avoid a risk which, although significant to you, can easily be coped with by them because of their expertise in that area. If this route is to be followed, contractual terms will have to underline the supplier's responsibility, and the team will need to consider the residual risk of the supplier failing in this respect.

Control

The planning process can be used to help you both identify risks *and* establish the means for testing them out before they can make an impact on the development. For example, the need for critical experiments, prototyping etc. can be established and these can then be carried out early enough in the project for alternative solutions to be sought in the case of failure.

Good management control will be required in any case. The day to day monitoring by management of the technical progress of the project allows problems to be spotted early enough for remedial action to be taken. Chapter 7 introduces some specific control actions that can be taken.

Insure

It is possible to take out insurance against certain forms of risk, eg supplier failure, or risks such as loss of or damage to critical equipment. Other risk elements such as product liability or professional indemnity insurance, or government guarantees (such as ECGD) which can be used to minimise financial exposure to customers who are in other countries, are not normally available to in-house developers of technical products.

Residual risk

What risk remains needs more drastic action: this might include changing the scope of the project or modifying the objectives. This is very common in the feasibility stage of development, and can be seen as a natural part of the process—the compromise between what the market would like and what can be developed at an acceptable cost and risk. Otherwise the scope could be changed, eg to establish whether a risk exists via research and experimentation, with no commitment to product development until this is known.

Competitive pressures for these technical risks to be taken are increasing, and companies are increasingly having to adopt 'simultaneous engineering' to shorten time scales—a technique which in itself increases risk by assuming the outcome from one area of development before starting another. This is a subject in its own right and will be dealt with in more detail later in this chapter.

Scenario planning To cope with residual risks, the technique of *scenario planning* may be helpful. This involves envisaging likely outcomes (or alternative scenarios) from whatever is causing the uncertainty. Some of the possible scenarios may be considered so unlikely that they can be discarded. The others should be 'fleshed out' to describe all the relevant circumstances that might pertain should they happen.

The next step is to plan for each of these scenarios. This should be done in some detail—arguably in as much detail as if each were the real situation (limiting the number of possible scenarios you can cope with). For each one, you must ask 'What would we have to do if this were the case?' and plan realistically for the situation.

Through analysing the resulting plans, you will find common threads and strategies that, although developed for one scenario, are actually suitable for others. You will then be in a position to choose the combination of development paths and strategies that are good solutions to the largest number of scenarios.

Contingency planning Another technique to cope with residual risk is to lay down contingency plans. This is somewhat akin to the above, except that there are not necessarily any common threads to the plans, or any common development strategies. However, it is still helpful to lay down your 'what if' plans ahead of the event. In this way you are able to both react more swiftly in the event, and by thinking the possible solution through in advance, you are better able to apply a calm rational approach to both the plans and the resulting action.

One of the early tasks a newly formed NPD team should undertake is the appraisal of risk in the above way. Following this framework, a 'risk management' plan should be developed by the team (see Figure 3.1).

Risk	Prob'y.[1]	Sev'y.[2]	Imp.[3]	Actions

Notes: [1]Probability of this risk occurring, expressed as a percentage, chance out of 10 etc.
[2]Severity measured in financial impact, scale of 1–10 etc.
[3]Relative importance, normally the product of the above two.

Figure 3.1 Risk management plan

A summary of some of the potential actions that could arise from this is given in the risk control checklist later in this chapter.

CONTAINING RISK

The traditional way in which risk has been managed is to limit the company's commitment depending on the scale of uncertainty faced—a technique known as *phased product development*. Although, as we shall examine later, this can have the effect of slowing a project down if it is badly implemented, an understanding of the development life cycle is a vital part of managing risk.

Product development often starts with 'just an idea', which may come from any number of sources, including:

- customer requests

- market research

- new or refined technological capability

- a purposeful analysis of the existing product range—*gap analysis*.

Whatever the source, the end result must meet customer requirements, produce profit for the company etc. Given that getting from idea to product available for sale is very often going to cost the company a significant expenditure of resources (man-power and money), how can the risks inherent in this be controlled?

Part of the answer lies in the adoption of a phased approach, where the commitment is limited at any one time, and development only proceeds if the risk assessed for the subsequent phase is commensurate with the amount being put at risk. The phases can be viewed in a variety of ways; the following gives a general overview.

Pre-development activity

As has been discussed in Chapter 1, in order for product development to be effective, a great deal of work is required that is relevant to many aspects of the company as well as to many projects, not just to one development. Part of the process must, therefore, be these 'pre-development' activities that lead to a clear definition of the company's view of the development objectives (steps 1 and 2 of the product definition process outlined in Chapter 1).

Concept definition

The original 'idea' needs to be converted into a clear definition of what is to be achieved by the development and why. This important phase, very often overlooked, is needed to:

- lay down the aims of the project, including the marketing objectives;

- stimulate clearer thinking and the rigorous initial appraisal of ideas using an agreed framework and common format;

- delineate at an early stage what the overall success criteria will be, and force the originator to examine aspects that may be outside his or her own discipline. It is vital to include technical, marketing and commercial objectives in the concept specification;

- provide a benchmark that will be invaluable in the later, often very complicated, phases of the project. When faced with difficult decisions and overwhelmed by details, it can be very helpful to look back on what was originally envisaged.

In terms of the product definition process outlined in Chapter 2, concept definition might include step 3—QFD (in outline form—detailed refinement would occur later), and possibly part of step 4 (concept development).

Evaluation

This will normally have multiple strands, including the best assessment of market and technical feasibility of the product concept that is possible at this stage. This will then allow a commercial judgement to be made of whether it is justified to continue with development, taking into account feasible costs and time scales. To enable this, step 4 of the definition process (concept development) must be complete and research may be used to test initial acceptability of options (data gathered during this can be used during specification).

For many products, especially technological ones, it is obvious that absolute feasibility cannot be established without significant expenditure of effort, arguably even until the end result is achieved in some cases! The company must therefore establish the right balance between expenditure of effort at this stage and the risk involved. The high number of technical developments that fail either before completion or at launch, would seem to indicate that more effort is generally required at this stage.

Specification

It is vital to define precisely what is required, separately from trying to do it. This normally has three aspects:

1. A definition of what the market requires in whatever detail and in the terms important to them. It is obviously desirable to define *only* what is important and to indicate areas of development options.
2. A definition of what the technology is capable of providing.
3. An agreement between the above two on exactly what is to be embodied in the product. This may involve compromise and further research, development of prototypes etc.

These activities would normally include QFD in detail, plus steps 5 and 6 of the definition process (determining customer value and product optimisation) in Chapter 1. Note: step 7—develop the product—is just a place marker for everything else that follows.

Clearly this phase involves the expenditure of significant effort. It should also be obvious that there might be irreconcilable differences that cause the project to be abandoned or radically altered at this stage.

Design and development

These are often, and quite justifiably, split into two stages. First, to sort out how the specification is to be implemented; secondly, actually doing it. These are best kept within one phase in this context as there is little justification for a formal commercial review between design and development. If the previous stages have been carried out correctly it must be possible to design it!

During this phase it is normal to include the production of pre-production prototypes for technical trials and market research.

Production ramp-up

Aspects of this will overlap with the previous phase. The detail required will vary, but the concept is common, involving tooling, the set-up of production control details, purchasing of parts, materials, documentation etc. 'Production' itself may involve just the duplication of software onto the appropriate media, but these other aspects will also normally be present.

Launch

The details of a launch would occupy a separate book on their own, but they can be broken down into four areas (the '4 Ps' of the marketing mix):

1. **Product**: Packaging, installation and support systems, warranty provisions, name, internal stock codes etc.
2. **Price**: Setting end-user prices, trade prices, discount structures, support pricing, printing new price lists etc.
3. **Place**: Warehousing, distributorships, dealerships, retailers, VARs, geographic coverage etc.
4. **Promotion**: Publicity, advertising, point of sale material, sales force (recruitment, training, incentives etc.), exhibitions etc.

The planning and preparation for all of this *must* be carried out prior to this point, perhaps in parallel with design and development. This phase is therefore the implementation of these actions.

Project reviews

Implicit in splitting the overall process into these phases is the fact that the process can be halted or abandoned at the end of any phase. The need to review earlier work should also be allowed for, eg there will always be the need to change the specification as a result of new market information or problems found during implementation. In the above context this should result in the project 'regressing' to the appropriate stage, and whatever management decisions required by the company being re-assessed.

These phases are discussed again in Chapter 6 which describes how teams need to be structured differently according to each phase of development.

Management scope

We can now address the issue of the scope of project management. Significant advantage can be gained by integrating the management across the above phases. In the extreme case, the same manager would be responsible for all phases, providing both continuity and perfect clarity of objectives. However, for many reasons this is not always possible, and in this situation various questions need to be addressed. How far in this direction is it possible to go? How will the handover points be managed? How will success be judged and how will this be made to reflect company success? These are all corporate, rather than project management decisions, but project managers must understand their role in the overall process and the implications of the above.

TIME TO MARKET

Although individual companies and projects will vary, in most cases the risk that the product might fail to sell is probably the worst of all possible consequences. In the introduction we touched briefly on the relative importance of three other ways in which development projects can fail (Table 3.1).

Table 3.1 Development projects—reason for failure

Cause	Impact on profits
Delayed launch	Severe
Incorrect quality	Moderate
Development costs too high	Minor

This highlights the fact that the speed of developing and launching new products has become of crucial importance. It is worth looking in more detail at the issues that affect this speed—known as 'time to market'.

Time to market should be the critical measure of a company's NPD efficiency—as the statistics show, the old measure of development cost bears little relationship to the bottom line. Time to market is not an absolute measure with some universally accepted definition —different companies (even within the same group) use different starting and end points, making simple inter-company comparisons impossible. One definition that has been put forward is 'the time taken from the earliest point at which the project *could* have started to the product being available to customers in the required volume'. This could be used as a measure within a single company to test for performance improvement, but would still be open to so much interpretation as to make inter-company comparisons impossible.

It is not the purpose of this book to deal extensively with this subject (particularly when it has been dealt with exhaustively in other works*), but no book on product development would be complete without a summary of the main issues and techniques.

The starting point is to consider the almost universally discredited technique of NPD project organisation, known as 'over the wall development'. This is based on traditional company structures, where a development project is conceived in one department and handed on 'over the wall' to other departments in turn (Figure 3.2).

Resources \ Phase	Concept	Design & development	Design validation	Production development & ramp-up
Marketing & product planning	▓▓▓			
Engineering		▓▓▓		
QA & test			▓▓▓	
Manufacturing				▓▓▓

*Smith and Reinertsen (1991) *Developing Products in Half the Time*, Van Nostrand Reinhold, New York.

The problems with developments managed in this way are due to the fact that they are both *compartmentalised* (each department acting autonomously) and *sequential* (little or no overlap between departments and phases). These problems manifest themselves as:

- objectives poorly defined and even lost as they are handed on;

- lost customer focus;

- nobody in overall control—no sense of ownership;

- very poor communications between phases and departments;

- lots of changes late in the process;

- expensive and slow.

Whilst there are probably very few companies still following this model slavishly, the philosophy that underlies it—that each department contributes autonomously—is still widespread in the West. The alternative approach (pioneered by the Japanese motor industry) is to break down the traditional departmental organisation structure and to carry out as many of these activities as possible in parallel. This has become known as 'simultaneous engineering' (SE) or—mainly in the USA—'concurrent engineering' (CE). These terms are rather unfortunate because they serve to reinforce the notion that product development is fundamentally an engineering function. One of the largest benefits of the approach described in this book is the integration of many disciplines, but especially the effective union of marketing into the process. This is why the term 'integrated product development' is used throughout this book. A simplified picture of this approach is given in Figure 3.3.

The benefits that accrue from IPD arise from the fact that it is quintessentially **integrated** (barriers between the disciplines must be broken down) *and* **simultaneous** (as many activities as possible overlapping). The benefits include:

- reduced time to market;

- clear definition of the goals from the beginning;

- effort can be put in at the right time—much earlier than normal;

- late changes are discouraged—efficiency is increased;

- teams are empowered and highly motivated.

Studies of the use of these practices in the motor industry* show that total development lead times, from the start of the concept study through to the start of continuous manufacture, average 63

*Hartley and Mortimer (1991) *Simultaneous Engineering*, Industrial Newsletters Ltd, Dunstable UK.

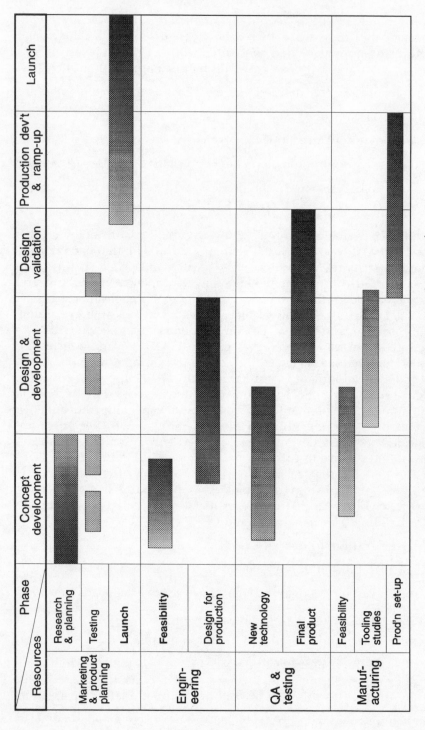

Figure 3.3 Integrated product development

months in Europe (using over the wall techniques) and 43 months
in Japan (using integrated techniques). Further improvements are
being made all the time as experience with the techniques speeds
the process further.

Improving time to market

The main techniques that have been used effectively to reduce time
to market include:

- Assemble a core multi-disciplinary team early in order to maintain a consistent vision of the goals.

- Ensure that the different strands of activity (traditionally the different disciplines) take place in parallel.

- Make sure that information is *pulled* from early activities by
  those needing it for later activities, ie the recipient of information
  (or any other output) is given greater importance—even regarded
  as the customer for each task. Their need for information (and
  other earlier outputs) should determine the priority of earlier
  tasks. This may well involve assembling a team much larger
  than would be normal from an early stage. Providing that it is
  correctly balanced, the needs of those who would normally only
  be included later can pull forward the results they need in order
  to be able to make progress themselves.

- Encourage the use of *partial information*. Efficient and open
  communications coupled with a high degree of trust within the
  team should enable people to start activities before the prior
  tasks are fully complete (where the technical risks involved
  allow this). For example, documents that need to be signed-off
  by a number of people can be circulated in draft form so the
  slow process of getting up to speed can take place off the critical
  path. Final sign-off can then take place after approving only the
  amendments.

- Use these techniques to ensure that as much individual task
  overlap takes place as is reasonably possible. Make sure the risks
  involved in high degrees of overlap are assessed and a balanced
  view is taken on how much overlap is used.

- If phased product development is being used for large scale risk
  management, organise to allow fuzzy phase ends so activity does
  not completely stop during the review process. Make sure that
  phase approval procedures operate smoothly and fast. Ensure
  that approval criteria are well understood by the team.

- Empower the development team to make as many decisions as

possible without needing to go outside the team. This will be made possible through the inclusion of staff from all the relevant disciplines as well as 'management heavyweights' (see Chapter 4).

- Don't try to follow other company's blueprints for IPD—develop your own interpretation whilst following the principles.

- Adopt incremental development whenever possible.

Incremental development

It makes sense that developments that deliver more are likely to take longer. In fact, this effect can be dramatic, with small problems compounding each other to make one very large, slow, late development. This is the large development trap (Figure 3.4).

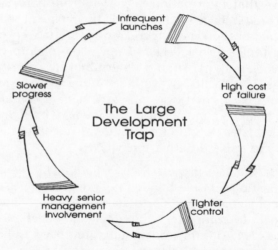

Figure 3.4 The large development trap

Large development projects suffer from a number of problems:

- They are slow to react to changes in market.

- Feedback from users becomes slow, resulting in lost opportunities to learn from your mistakes.

- There is compound growth in the interactions between product elements and team members (a team of three has three possible person to person interactions, a team of ten has 45!). Every interaction will require managing in one form or another.

- The larger the project the larger the learning burden for the whole team (unless the project is compartmentalised with all the problems that can bring).

- Large projects can become glamorous in their own right. This causes concentration on the project but not what it is trying to achieve.

- Large developments are often caused by trying to compete with *all* competitors' product features or by 'leaping to an unassailable lead', rather than optimising the match between the product and its market which is more efficient and less risky.

- They make technology too visible—customers want the benefits, not the technology *per se*.

- Customers' expectations may be raised—often beyond the product's ability to perform.

- They give fast competitors an advantage—by learning from *your* experience!

The alternative to this is to adopt an approach known as *incremental development*. This is to make frequent small changes to products to keep them abreast of customer requirements and available technology, and is only possible if the company has a well developed long-term plan for its products and markets (see Chapter 1).

The word 'frequent' should be taken in context. In some industries (notably personal computer software) the pressures to keep improving the product can be strong, but are balanced by the complexities of supporting a large number of similar versions and the danger that existing owners will become dissatisfied by the thought that they have recently bought something that is now out of date. Under these circumstances, management will have to take a carefully balanced view to avoid the large development trap without incurring these problems.

GOAL RECONCILIATION

We have concentrated on the subject of reducing time to market for some very good reasons, including:

- Market share may be lost irretrievably to the competition and sales may be slow to build thereafter.

- High costs of development expense and inventory, plus interest on these.

- Disruption to production plans and subsequent efficiency losses.

- Loss of morale within the team.

- Lost opportunity and reduced return on capital employed due to under-utilised capacity, and development costs incurred earlier than expected sales.

- May need to improve features or lower price to compete.

However, even though a shorter development time is very likely to bring an increase in life-cycle profits, it may also mean:

- a more expensive development (see Chapter 7, page 172, Figure 7.5; or

- reduced features; or

- higher end-user costs (less time for value engineering, see Chapter 2, page 73, Figure 2.2).

Another frequently observed pressure from sales and marketing departments is to add more features or to sell for a lower end-user price. This may produce a lower risk of market failure (see page 84), *but* it will also produce a longer and more expensive development project, or reduced margins.

These examples illustrate the fact that there are four separate dimensions that need to be controlled and traded-off against each other during NPD. These are:

1. Product quality (ie all elements of the 'total product');
2. Product cost;
3. Time to market;
4. Development cost.

We have seen from the above points that the interactions between these dimensions are complex. To be able to make sensible decisions, they need to be prioritised, or preferably converted into some common format that allows trade-offs between them to take place.

The obvious choice for a common means of comparison is money. To allow comparison, the impact on company profits will have to be calculated for any potential trade-off. This is relatively straightforward for development cost and product cost (assuming no confusion exists between product cost and price charged). For the other dimensions however the calculations are more difficult.

In the product quality dimension, any change will result in:

- a changed value to the purchaser, resulting from price comparisons being made with alternative and substitute products. You will need to set a different selling price to compensate for this.

- a changed market share for the same reasons.

- some combination of these, where both price and market share will change.

If the change in quality being considered is the removal of a feature that was properly researched in the product definition process, the profit impact of the above can be calculated from the preference model (see Chapter 2, 'Feature/Benefit optimisation'). Otherwise, best estimates of these effects must be made by those able to make them (this may be marketing, product planning or some other group within the company).

The time-to-market dimension is undeniably the most difficult to quantify in terms of its impact on profitability. Although it is commonly regarded as being very important, it is vital that you understand the effect in *your* company before making any trade-off decisions. It would be folly to rely on someone else's formula.

The following factors should be considered:

- Lost sales during the delay.

- Whether this results in permanently lost sales or merely delayed sales.

- Lost market share due to these early lost sales. This could be a major effect if you believe you are in a race with the competition—the first to market often retains market leadership against all comers.

To allow comparisons to be made, a model of the financial performance will have to be constructed. This can be done using simple spreadsheet tools with the following inputs (initially using baseline or originally planned data):

1. Forecast sales volumes over the expected product life. This in turn may be calculated from market share and market size, each of which may vary with time.
2. Planned product pricing over its expected life.
3. Forecast product cost and its variation over product life.
4. The relationship between product cost and volume.
5. Development costs (including tooling) and their timing.
6. Marketing costs (including launch) and their timing.

The spreadsheet can now be set up to calculate cash flow, breakeven point and profitability. The impact on each of these coming from potential changes to development cost, time to market, product cost or product quality can now be assessed and the appropriate decisions made on a rational basis.

RISK CONTROL CHECKLIST

- Adopt incremental product development. Small developments to the product or movements into near markets are always less risky as there is less uncertainty.

- Be flexible. If you can identify a source of risk, develop a fall back position and, if possible, adopt a design architecture which allows a final choice of solution when the outcome of the risk is known.

- Research the market to clarify critical product parameters sufficiently early in the development.

- Use experts for their disciplines. Avoid the temptation to 'have a go at' someone else's area of expertise which, from a distance, can often look easier than it really is. This applies as much to marketing disciplines (research, strategy, planning etc.) as it does to areas of engineering, design and management.

- Involve customers in your teams. Either involve key representative customers or use frequent market tests during development. See Chapters 1 and 5 for details of how to achieve this.

- Make sure that areas of high risk are kept highly visible. Identify them early and review them often.

- Allow and encourage maximum communication within the team (see Chapter 5). Spend time 'wandering around' to find out what people are doing and what their worries are. Get them to test their assumptions with each other at all times.

- Make sure that the team includes all relevant disciplines and that they are well integrated into the team (see Chapter 4). See also the above on using experts.

- Don't shoot the bringer of bad tidings. Positively encourage someone to take on the role of team 'Jonah' (but allow the role to rotate amongst the team).

- Test all assumptions as early as possible.

- Remember that testing applies to marketing risks and technical risks alike.

- Maintain contingency plans. A plan is a living thing, and a contingency plan which is not maintained is probably useless.

- Consider parallel development routes. The cost of developing two (or more) alternate technical solutions to a particular problem may be very great, so this route should only be chosen if the probability and severity of a single solution failing is high enough to justify the cost.

- Produce models and test them. Models can start as mathematical constructs or on a computer—this can be an extremely effective and cheap means of early testing. However nothing is as effective as a real model—this can be a non-functioning space model for user reaction, a 'rapid prototype' for software or a bread-board for electronics.

• Avoid using models that were designed to test for technical risk for market testing as well—the requirements are often very different.

In conclusion, it is worth looking at the following analogy. The traditional view of NPD is rather like carving up a stick of rock (the British seaside variety that has a message running through it) lengthways—a large deliverable is split into parts that make no sense on their own (Figure 3.5).

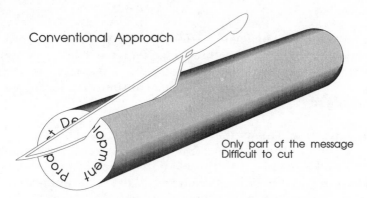

Conventional Approach

Only part of the message
Difficult to cut

Figure 3.5 NPD—the conventional approach

However, Figure 3.6 demonstrates the more logical approach to NPD—the overall deliverable is reduced to smaller, more manageable sections, each of which is complete and makes sense in its own right (Figure 3.6)!

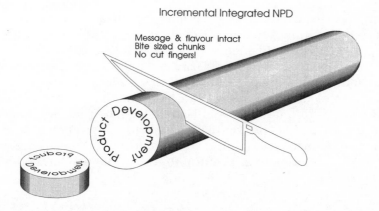

Incremental Integrated NPD

Message & flavour intact
Bite sized chunks
No cut fingers!

Figure 3.6 NPD—the integrated and incremental approach

4

Team Building

INTRODUCTION

Team work is the mechanism for achieving integrated product development. In the next three chapters we take a pragmatic approach and spell out some of the specific steps that result in good team work. Let's be clear about the use of some key terms we will be using here.

Team building: This is the set of actions that allows a working group to achieve the quality of integrated work that can genuinely be described as team work. There are five crucial steps involved in team building that in our experience lead to successful team work. This is the subject covered in this chapter.

Team work: This is the state you are aiming for when you want a range of different people to contribute to a common goal. It is characterised by co-operative effort and co-ordinated by clear leadership. The processes involved in working as a true team are covered in Chapter 5.

Team development: This describes the phases that a working team will naturally progress through, partly as a function of time and partly as a consequence of the team building actions. Since the way teams are structured should vary with the stage of their development, the whole topic of team structures is covered in chapter 6.

The aim of these chapters is to help anyone involved in new product development to recognise what can be done to integrate the resources, effort and goodwill needed to achieve timely success in the market place. These three topics of team building, team work and team development are central to this whole way of working.

TEAM BUILDING

If team work is the state you aspire to for successful new product development, then team building is the process you need to work through to get there.

It is worth removing one common misapprehension about what team building is. We are sometimes told 'I would love to do some team building to get this project up and running, but we have a recruitment freeze on right now, and there is no chance of getting any new people in. I have to make do with the team I've got'. Team building is not primarily about bringing in new people, although this may become a part of it. Nor is it about making do with the team you have. Rather it is about taking active steps to make the most of the team you have.

We need to think further about team membership. In integrated product development we are invariably talking about multi-disciplinary teams, made up of individuals with different technical training and experience from across the company's different functions—technical, manufacturing, marketing, product support and so on, all working together rather than in sequence. For more on this subject refer back to Chapter 3, 'Time to market'.

Another important distinction to make is between the core team and the extended team. The core team is usually made up of people working full time on the project, who are located in the same space (co-located). The extended team consists of the other people on whom the success of the project relies: people who contribute part-time to the project from inside or outside the company; third parties; subcontractors; suppliers; customers; dealers.

The bulk of direct team building work will be restricted to the core team, for practical reasons. However, one of the best lessons that team members can learn is to apply some of the principles to the extended team where appropriate.

Our experience in front line work with project teams and people involved with new product development has led us to identify five crucial steps to the process of team building:

1. Understand your goal;
2. Know yourself;
3. Get to know the other team members;
4. Work out the roles and responsibilities in the team—who will do what?;
5. Establish the ground rules—how will you work together?

Working through these steps is not a one-off process. You will find yourselves developing aspects of each step as you go through the project cycle. But the first time you work through them, all five steps should be organised as a special session. You should run this as early as possible once a new team has been formed, or a new project begun. Ideally you should set aside two days and get away from your regular work environment. The detail that follows on the five steps should help you to organise the session.

STEP 1: UNDERSTAND YOUR GOAL

The theme of the three perspectives that was outlined in the introductory chapter and runs through this book—the customer, the company and the team—is perhaps nowhere so important as it is in understanding your goal.

What is the goal from the customer's perspective? You need to ask yourselves this kind of question to make sure that you can answer these major ones:

- Who is the customer?

- Who else might be a customer?

- What does the customer really want?

- What does the customer value?

- Are we reviewing possible changes in customer requirements often enough?

- What is the goal from the company's perspective?

We covered some aspects of these topics in Chapter 1 in the section on 'Market focus'.

For the purposes of opening your team building session, you should be asking yourselves the following kinds of questions:

- Where does this project fit in the company's overall strategic direction?

- Where does it fit in with the company's product strategy?

- Where does it fit in with the company's marketing strategy?

- What is the criterion for success in this project from the company's viewpoint?

- What will success with this project mean to the company and its future?

We then need to move on and ask: What is the goal from the team's perspective? This subject was also mentioned briefly in the introductory chapter. What you need to consider here, individually and jointly, are some of the following issues:

- Can every one of you say clearly what the project goal is?

- Can you write the goal down and all agree with the wording?

- Does the goal make sense to you?

- Is the goal clear and elevating (see above)?

- Do you believe that the goal is achievable and realistic?

- Can you raise this project goal above your personal priorities if needs be?

By definition a project sets out to achieve a specific goal. This is one of the features that differentiates it from other kinds of work. Although this is not so well documented, having a common goal is also part of the definition of a team, and probably the main feature that differentiates a team from other working groups.

STEP 2: KNOW YOURSELF

The second practical step in team building is for each member of the team, including and especially the team leader, to develop their own self-insight. To be able to make a real contribution on a project team you need to know a great deal about yourself, your nature, your way of working, your strengths and your weaknesses.

This is a big subject, and not one that everyone relishes putting time into. But take heart, there are limits to this quest for self-insight. The reason for taking this as the second step is that for present purposes you need to get to know *yourself* relative to the project goal. What do you bring to the team that will help to achieve the goal? Are you a technical wizard? Do you have special creative powers? Are you good at handling the kinds of interpersonal conflicts that frequently arise in working teams? Can you organise and control things—achieve order out of chaos?

Here are some guidelines for this step in the team building process:

- Consider what your natural style of relating to people is. Are you reserved, gregarious, group orientated, self-sufficient? There is usually no need to change your style—just make sure the team gets the best you can offer.

- Whatever your style, work to adopt helpful behaviour in a team environment. Show commitment and enthusiasm. Listen to the others. Be available to them. Participate in discussions.

- Make a conscious effort to play an active part in the team's life for every project team you are involved in.

- If you are a natural cynic, think before you speak, and consider what will be achieved by your comments before you make them.

- Encourage other people in the team to give you feedback on your performance and behaviour—both technical and in terms of group participation. Learning from each other is one of the best opportunities provided by working in teams.

- Are you the right person to be doing your job in the project?

- If you have some genuine concerns about your capability to make a contribution to the project then the appropriate thing to do is talk to your line manager or personnel manager.

To get really into the spirit of team work, your own personal goal should be to waste no opportunity that the project offers you. That way, the chances are that you will have something more to offer to the next project you take part in.

There are several psychometric questionnaires that can help to develop your self-insight by letting you see how you compare with peers on a range of personality variables such as communication style, style of decision making, and the degree to which you like to have things controlled and organised, or left open and flexible. The *Myers Briggs Type Indicator* is one questionnaire that we find particularly valuable in this context.

STEP 3: GET TO KNOW THE OTHER TEAM MEMBERS

You may find yourself working with people you have had no contact with before. There is a lot of information to be shared about one another before you will be able to work as a team. Here are some suggestions that will help you understand the kind of people they are:

- What are their backgrounds and experiences? What are they hoping for out of life, now and in the future? What other interests do they have outside work?

- What do they think their best achievements have been in the past?

- Do they need help in getting involved in meetings and other discussions and what do they find most helpful?

- In the section 'Know yourself' we suggested you encourage other people to give you feedback. Here is your opportunity to reciprocate. Be observant. Care about how your fellow team members are doing, and be prepared to give them feedback from your observations in working alongside them.

You may be thrown together with someone you have worked with before and not got on with at all. If you are to make the best of the opportunities this project can provide then you need to work out your problems with this person early on. Acknowledge that you have had difficulties and check the other person's perception of what the problems have been in the past. Take time to discuss these past differences without indulging too much. Then move on purposefully to work out ways in which you can avoid future disagreements and set shared objectives for the project work you will both be involved with.

Role negotiation

Once the team is working, there is a useful technique known as *role negotiation* that can help people learn more about themselves through other team members. You can use this as part of team building where team members have experience of working together, though it is rather time consuming to be a feasible part of the initial team building session.

Role negotiation is a genuine negotiation—working out an agreement between pairs of people to achieve a better working relationship. There are three parts to the exercise. In preparation, both team members need to think about each of the following with reference to the behaviour of the other person:

- three things I would like you to go on doing;
- three things I would like you to do less of;
- three things I would like you to do more of.

Having done this preparation, the pairs get together to talk reciprocally through the needs they have of the other person.

An example may help to bring the process to life. John and Paul went through the exercise to prepare themselves for an overseas trip on project business that was going to throw the two of them together rather more than they cared for. This was John's side of the negotiation, expressing his requirements of Paul:

- *go on being friendly;*
- *go on being organised;*
- *go on being considerate of the need for time off.*

- *less talking about business;*
- *less saying 'that's OK';*
- *less saying 'let me walk you through this'.*

- *show more awareness of other people's needs—be more tactful;*
- *laugh more;*
- *be more relaxed.*

These were Paul's needs of John:

- *continue with the high level of professionalism and quality standards in the work you do;*
- *go on showing me the respect and trust that has always been mutual in our work together;*
- *go on being tolerant of the difficult circumstances we often find ourselves in when we're travelling.*

- *less up-tight behaviour if any of our travel arrangements go wrong beyond my control;*
- *make fewer critical comments—especially watch out for the timeliness of your comments;*
- *don't be so defensive about what you perceive as criticism from me.*

- *pay more attention to the milestones that are set in the project plan;*
- *take more advantage of rest opportunities during our travel schedules;*
- *take more care in setting up for interviews.*

By the time Paul and John had talked through these issues in a free and frank exchange of views they certainly understood one another a lot better! The process may sound a bit daunting, but it should be taken in a reasonably light-hearted way without trivialising it, and it can be extremely constructive in building lasting relationships.

Team roles

One of the most useful analytical tools to help team members understand each other is the *Belbin Team Role Inventory*. After years of intensive research into working teams, British psychologist Meredith Belbin has identified nine different roles that can be adopted by team members. He has developed a set of questions that help people identify which of these roles comes naturally to them and which they should best avoid.

Belbin's main argument is that people at work have a dual role. The first is functional, eg software engineer, accountant, etc. The second is the natural style people adopt when they work alongside others. Belbin calls these team roles.

The following descriptions are extracted from Belbin's *Interplace*.*

Plant

Characteristics: Plants are innovators and inventors and can be highly creative. They provide the seeds and ideas from which major developments spring. Usually they prefer to operate by themselves at some distance from the other members of the team, using their imagination and often working in an unorthodox way. They tend to be introverted and react strongly to criticism and praise. Their ideas may often be radical and may lack practical constraint. They are independent, clever and original, but may be weak in communicating with other people on a different wave length.

Function: The main use of a Plant is to generate new proposals and to solve complex problems. Plants are often needed in the initial stages of a project or when a project is failing to progress. Plants have usually made their mark as founders of companies or as originators of new products. Too many Plants in one organisation, however, may be counter-productive as they tend to spend their time reinforcing their own ideas and engaging each other in combat.

Resource Investigator

Characteristics: Resource Investigators (RIs) are often enthusiastic, quick-off-the-mark extroverts. They are good at communicating with people both inside and outside the company. They are natural negotiators and are adept at exploring new opportunities and developing contacts. Although not a great source of new ideas, the RI is effective when it comes to picking up other people's ideas and developing them. As the name suggests, they are skilled at finding out what is available and what can be done. They usually receive a warm reception from others because of their own outgoing nature. RIs have relaxed personalities with a strong inquisitive sense and a readiness to see the possibilities in anything new. However, unless they remain stimulated by others, their enthusiasm rapidly fades.

Function: RIs are good at exploring and reporting back on ideas, developments or resources outside the group. They are the best people to set up external contacts and to carry out any subsequent negotiations. They have an ability to think on their feet and to probe others for information.

---

*Used with permission from Belbin Associates, Cambridge.

Co-ordinator

Characteristics: The distinguishing feature of Co-ordinators is their ability to cause others to work towards shared goals. Mature, trusting and confident, they delegate readily. In interpersonal relations they are quick to spot individual talents and to use them in the pursuit of group objectives. While Co-ordinators are not necessarily the cleverest members of a team, they have a broad and worldly outlook and generally command respect.

Function: Co-ordinators are well placed when put in charge of a team of people with diverse skills and personal characteristics. They perform better in dealing with colleagues of near or equal rank than in directing junior subordinates. Their motto might well be 'consultation with control' and they usually believe in tackling problems calmly.

Shaper

Characteristics: Shapers are highly motivated people with a lot of nervous energy and a great need for achievement. Usually they are aggressive extroverts and possess strong drive. Shapers like to challenge others and their concern is to win. They like to lead and to push others into action. If obstacles arise, they will find a way round them. Headstrong and assertive, they tend to show strong emotional response to any form of disappointment or frustration. Shapers are single minded and argumentative and may lack interpersonal understanding. Theirs is the most competitive team role.

Function: Shapers generally make good managers because they generate action and thrive under pressure. They are excellent at sparking life into a team and are very useful in groups where political complications are apt to slow things down. Shapers are inclined to rise above problems of this kind and forge ahead regardless. They are well suited to making necessary changes and do not mind taking unpopular decisions. As the name implies, they try to impose some shape or pattern on group discussions or activities. They are probably the most effective members of a team in guaranteeing positive action. In some firms Co-ordinators are inclined to clash with Shapers due to their contrasting management styles.

Monitor evaluator

Characteristics: Monitor Evaluators (MEs) are serious-minded, prudent individuals with a built-in immunity from being over-enthusiastic. They are slow in making decisions, preferring to think things over. Usually they have a high critical thinking ability. They have a capacity for shrewd judgement that takes all factors into account. A good ME is seldom wrong.

Function: MEs are best suited to analysing problems and evaluating ideas and suggestions. They are very good at weighing up the pros and cons of options. To many outsiders the ME may appear as dry, boring or even over critical. Some people are surprised that they become managers. Nevertheless, many MEs occupy strategic posts and thrive in high level appointments. In some jobs success or failure hinges on a relatively small number of crunch decisions. This is ideal territory for an ME; for the person who is never wrong is the one who scores in the end.

Team worker

Characteristics: Team Workers (TWs) are the most supportive members of a team. They are mild, sociable and concerned about others. They have a great capacity for flexibility and adapting to different situations and people. TWs are perceptive and diplomatic. They are good listeners and are generally popular members of a group. They operate with a sensitivity at work, but they may be indecisive in crunch situations.

Features: The role of the TW is to prevent interpersonal problems arising within a team and thus allow all team members to contribute effectively. They will go to great lengths to avoid friction. It is not uncommon for TWs to become senior managers especially if line managers are dominated by Shapers. This creates a climate in which the diplomatic and perceptive skills of a TW become real assets, especially under a managerial regime where conflicts are liable to arise or to be artificially suppressed. TW managers are seen as a threat to no one and therefore the most accepted and favoured people to serve under. TWs have a lubricating effect on teams. Morale is better and people seem to co-operate better when they are around.

Implementer

Characteristics: Implementers (IMPs) have practical common sense and a good deal of self-control and discipline. They favour hard work and tackle problems in a systematic fashion. On a wider front, the IMP is typically a person whose loyalty and interest lie with the company and who is less concerned with the pursuit of self-interest. However, IMPs may lack spontaneity and show signs of rigidity.

Function: IMPs are useful to an organisation because of their reliability and capacity for application. They succeed because they are efficient and because they have a sense of what is feasible and relevant. It is said that many executives only do the jobs they wish to do and neglect those tasks which they find distasteful. By contrast, an IMP will do what needs to be done. Good IMPs often progress to high management positions by virtue of good organisational skills and competency in tackling necessary tasks.

Completer-finisher

Characteristics: Completer-Finishers (CFs) have a great capacity for follow-through and attention to detail. They are unlikely to start anything that they cannot finish. They are motivated by internal anxiety, yet outwardly they may appear unruffled. Typically they are introverted and require little in the way of external stimulus or incentive. CFs can be intolerant of those with a casual disposition. They are not often keen on delegating, preferring to tackle all tasks themselves.

Function: CFs are invaluable where tasks demand close concentration and a high degree of accuracy. They foster a sense of urgency within a team and are good at meeting schedules. In management they excel by the high standards to which they aspire and by their concern for precision, attention to detail and follow-through.

Specialist

 *Characteristics*: Specialists (SPs) are dedicated individuals who pride themselves on acquiring technical skills and specialised knowledge. Their priorities centre on maintaining professional standards and on furthering and defending their own field. While they show great pride in their own subject, they usually lack interest in other people's. Eventually, the SP becomes the expert by sheer commitment along a narrow front. There are few people who have either the single-mindedness or the aptitude to become a first-class SP.

Function: SPs have an indispensable part to play in some teams, for they provide the rare skill upon which the firm's service or product is based. As managers, they command support because they know more about their subject than anyone else and can usually be called upon to make decisions based on in-depth experience.

In conclusion

The aim is to have a good mix of the required skills and knowledge in the team members so that each one can make a full contribution. Having too little to contribute to a team is as stressful and destructive as having to do too much. The right balance of personality types can be achieved by careful assessment of individuals, teams and the task at hand. Homogeneity makes for stable, long-lasting teams, but these are not necessarily the most creative. A newcomer may upset the social cohesion of a team, but can also be a spur to progress. Heterogeneity makes for excellent productivity but increases the likelihood of conflict and breakdown. See, for example Chapter 3, 'Planning for risk'. Specific meetings and sub-goals can be approached with far greater chance of success if the make-up of the team is considered in advance.

There will be further reference to these team roles in Chapter 6 where we look at team structures at the different stages of product development.

STEP 4: WORK OUT YOUR CONTRIBUTION: ROLES AND RESPONSIBILITIES

Based on your understanding of the project goal, your knowledge about yourself and the other team members, the team is now ready to establish who will do what to achieve the goal. We are not talking here about tight job descriptions. There may be a place for these elsewhere in the company, but they are not in keeping with project team work. In place of job descriptions we talk about contributions to emphasise the fact that any team member is only one part of the whole, and also that the effort put into the project must be generously given. Each team member therefore has to make an offering of what you can best contribute. Ideally this will fall into three parts:

1. responsibilities for getting specific things done;
2. roles that describe your natural style of working;
3. commitment to bettering the overall team performance.

Let's look at each of these in some more detail.

Responsibilities

This is about the responsibility for specific aspects of the work that has to be done—in terms of actions, outputs and results. For example, here is a statement from a real project developing a new computer system: 'I am responsible for all the documentation that goes with this new product and its development. This certainly doesn't mean that I will write every word myself. What it does mean is that the project leader can count on me to have all the documentation ready on time and to the right standard in line with the project plan'.

Clearly this step of identifying responsibilities is very closely linked to the detail of your project plan. It is the human face of the plan, showing who will do what of all the activities broken down in the plan. There is an important link here with the planning process—see Chapter 7, 'A planning framework'. The work breakdown structures of traditional project planning need to be mapped on to real people with the right skills and working styles.

The technique of *responsibility charting* can help to show who is taking responsibility for which activities and can be used to double check that every action on the project plan has an owner. The chart (Figure 4.1) consists of activities listed down the left-hand side and each individual's name along the top. The codes below then indicate how each person will make their contribution.

> R = Responsibility for the activity;
> S = Provides support or resources for the activity;
> I = Needs to be informed about progress on the activity;
> A–V = The right to approve or veto a decision.

This technique also demonstrates how the fabric of the team is made up. If you take on a specific responsibility you should be able to rely on support from other named people in the core team or the extended team. You should know who to keep informed about progress on your activities, and should be clear about who has the right to approve or veto a particular action or decision. All of this information gets worked out on the responsibility chart, making it a very valuable group exercise at this stage in the team building process.

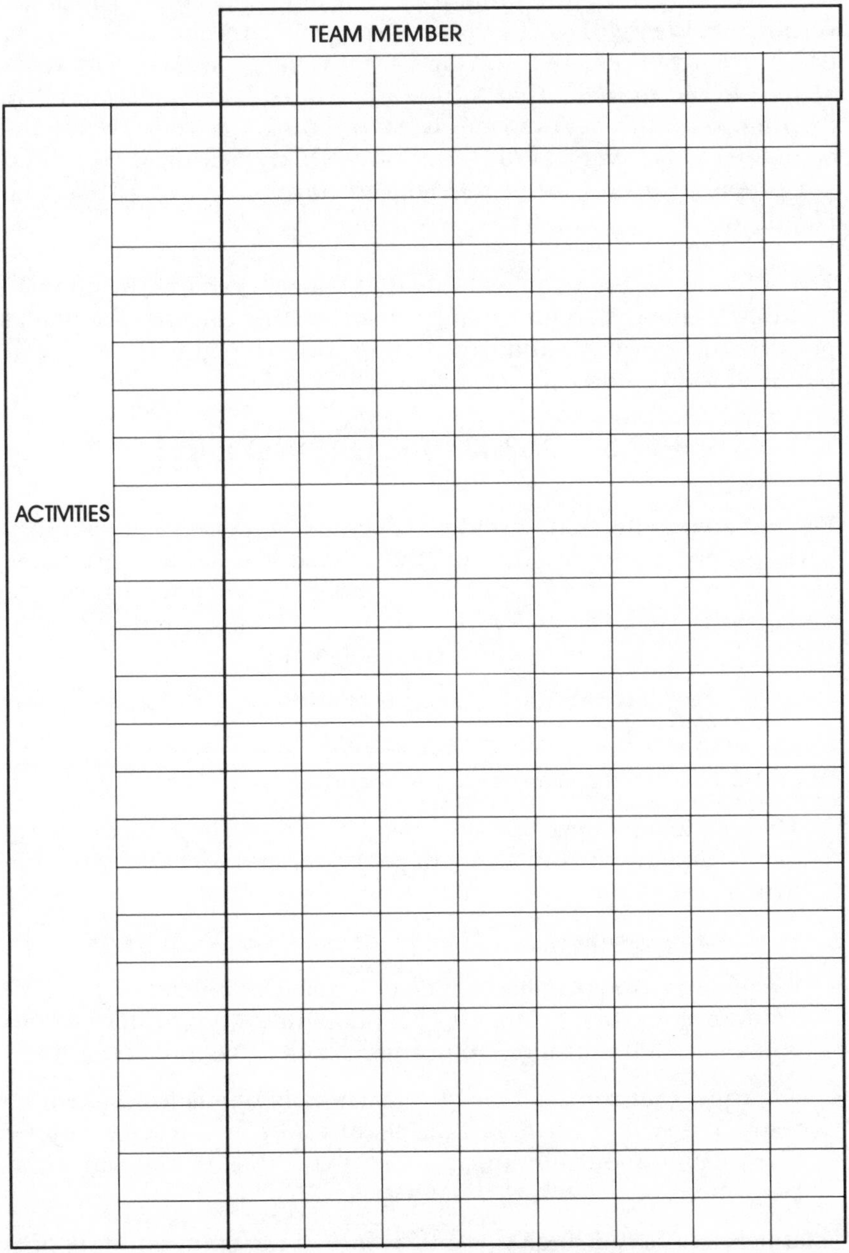

	TEAM MEMBER							
ACTIVITIES								

Figure 4.1 The responsibility chart

Roles

Your best role in the team fits in with your natural working style. Belbin's team roles, described earlier, have such power and are now so widely recognised that they have almost become part of the vernacular. We regularly hear people talking in these terms: 'I know I'm not a resource investigator. I really need someone to work alongside me to make the right kind of outside contacts that will help me keep the detail of my work on track. I'm your archetypal completer—all I want to do is get on with my technical work and I'm prepared to put in all the hours it takes to do this to a high standard'.

There has to be one responsibility that has to be shared by all team members. This is a commitment to contributing towards the team's performance overall and to pulling your weight in any way required to this end.

STEP 5: ESTABLISH THE GROUND RULES

The last step in the team building process is to decide between you how you are going to work together—what are the ground rules? Every team involved in integrated product development needs to establish its own. For illustration, here are some ground rules that project teams have devised for themselves:

- We will review monthly our understanding of the project goal.

- We will keep each other up to date informally as much as possible, and formally in a weekly status meeting.

- This is a team where it is safe to speak out and express disagreement—though we will all try to get better at doing this constructively.

- Wherever possible we will make decisions by consensus.

- We will not hide problems that could have an impact on the progress of the project—anyone can raise their own problems and we will treat them as group problems and solve them creatively.

- We know that some of our best learning happens from our mistakes. We will help the whole team effort of the company by being open about our mistakes so that other teams can learn from them.

Establishing ground rules is the fifth step of the team building process. Before you take this step you may like to read about the team processes described in the next chapter.

5

Team Working

INTRODUCTION

The first thing you need to know is what you are aiming for here. Will you recognise team work when you see it? We need to know the real characteristics of team work. Let's learn these from two different sources: research and plain experience.

Larson and Lafasto* conducted a thorough study of different kinds of teams and factored out those features that characterise the successful ones. These are the features they identified:

- A clear, elevating goal;

- A results-driven structure;

- Competent team members;

- Unified commitment;

- A collaborative climate;

- Standards of excellence;

- External support and recognition;

- Principled leadership.

It also helps to look back on our own experiences and use these as a benchmark for what we want to achieve in our team work. We have all had some experiences in the course of our lives that we can identify with team work. These will have been to do with sport, playing music, taking part in social or church groups, and even work!

Over the years we have collected hundreds of anecdotes about people's experiences in teams and what has made for a sense of

---

*Larson C E and Lafasto F M J (1989) *Teamwork—What must go right/what can go wrong*, Sage Publications, Newbury Park.

success, whatever the team was trying to achieve. Here are some of the regular items raised:

- togetherness—a feeling of companionship and good relations;

- trust and mutual support;

- being highly motivated to do the best you humanly can so as not to let the others down;

- not being afraid to speak out;

- whole-hearted commitment to what you are all trying to achieve;

- fun—real enjoyment and immersion in what you are doing to the exclusion (for the time being) of other things.

A valuable activity in the early days of a working team is to get everyone together informally and have a brainstorming session to get out your team's list of experiences. Get someone to write up the ideas as they emerge, and have the final list typed up as a record of what you are aiming to achieve in the quality of your team work.

In Chapter 4 we described the five steps of team building that help to get us toward the state of successful team working. In this chapter we look at team processes to give us some practical ideas about how teams can maintain and continue to improve the way they work together. Some aspects of these team processes may well find their way into your ground rules when you work through the fifth step of team building.

Elsewhere in the book we describe in detail the major aspects of new product development: goal setting, quality function deployment (QFD), risk assessment, planning and control. What we concentrate on here are the specific processes that your team should try to develop so that it can perform these core activities to the highest possible standards.

These are the ten team processes that we have found most valuable in achieving integrated product development:

1. Keeping informed
2. Managing change
3. Learning from each other
4. Encouraging the wider project team
5. An attitude of total quality
6. Leading and following
7. Problem solving
8. Conflict resolution
9. Decision making
10. Good communications.

KEEPING INFORMED

Teams involved in new product development need to keep themselves informed about what is happening in the outside world as well as keeping one another in touch with progress and events going on inside the project. Your third team building step will have identified the natural communication styles of people in the team.

Contact with the outside world

Your more extrovert, outgoing and communicative types are the people who should be trusted to make contacts with people in the outside world, with customers, suppliers, researchers, government departments, journalists—everyone who will keep you in touch with the real world as it affects your project.

The quieter, more studious people in the team can also contribute here through their reading of technical journals. They may need encouragement to communicate the relevant information to other people in the team. This can be done through short, regular get-togethers where key points are raised and discussed, supported perhaps by a summary sheet on the notice board near the coffee machine.

Chapter 3, Risk in NPD, provides guidelines for the sort of information you need to keep your project on track.

Team meetings

Teams do not work without meetings, however much people hate them. Make them as formal or informal as you please, but follow the rules:

Before the meeting

1. Be clear about the objectives of every meeting you hold. Likely options include:
    - reporting progress against the project plan (status reports);
    - communication of news and developments;
    - informing colleagues about problems and issues to get fresh outlooks, suggestions and contributions;
    - resolving technical issues;
    - fostering team spirit.
2. Decide who needs to attend and restrict attendance to these people. Only people who are currently active on the project need to be involved. This will result in a changing pattern of attendance.

3. Decide who should be briefed about the outcomes of the meeting.
4. Collect data on current progress and status from everyone working on the project. Update the plan to reflect this and prepare a summary report for the meeting. Prepare your thoughts on what corrective actions are needed.
5. Check action points from previous meeting. Be prepared to raise any outstanding items at the next meeting.

At the meeting

1. Start and finish on time, and keep meetings simple and short.
2. Check position on previously agreed action points (open items only).
3. Restrict minutes to actions/person responsible/time to be completed. It may be worth agreeing and even printing forms for the purpose. Every action should have a defined deliverable. Question any actions with no clear deliverable.
4. Discourage diversions from the subject. Agree policy before discussing detail.
5. Make sure everyone present has an opportunity to comment on each item.
6. Check at the end that the purpose of the meeting was achieved. If not, what corrective action can you take next time?
7. Agree date of next meeting.
8. Make sure that action minutes are circulated to everyone within the agreed time.

One of the prime sources of discontent about meetings is that nothing seems to happen. The form shown in Figure 5.1 could help change that. It is quite easy for everyone to see what must be done, but common for people to forget that someone has to do it. There has to be a deadline for actions otherwise the 'nothing happens' prediction becomes all too true.

The 'I' in responsibility charts

Outside regular meetings there should be a constant flow of information between team members. The 'I' category in the responsibility charts that were described in Chapter 4 will add some structure to this flow.

Meeting:			
Date:			
Action/Decision	**By whom**	**By when**	**Date done**
Project Manager's Signature:			

Figure 5.1 Action sheet

MANAGING CHANGE

Flexibility

What happens when priorities change and the project plan you have been working on for weeks simply does not fit any more? People differ in their capacity to tolerate change. Some team members will be as adaptable as can be, happy to switch their activities at a moment's notice. Others will find a change of direction extremely irritating and will resist vehemently any change to their own work schedule. You will have learned about these characteristics in the third step of team building, and knowing how people will react can take a lot of the difficulty out of the management of change.

Project leaders and team members have a particular need to work flexibly because of the interdisciplinary nature of integrated product development teams. The approach that a marketing person takes to a problem may be completely alien to a technician, but the only way these teams will work is if everyone is prepared to adapt to meet the immediate requirements, even if it does mean acting in a way that they have never tried before.

Judgements about making change

There are two important ingredients to ensuring good judgements about making change in project work.

1. **The relationship between the project leader and team members:** This must be sound, with enough respect to avoid time wasting and enough understanding to avoid fear. This kind of relationship will allow team members to make judgements that are within their capacity, yet speak up and ask for help when they need it.

   We saw another benefit recently where a project leader worked consciously to improve his relationships with team members. One of the quietest and most reserved individuals announced that he was currently under-employed and asked if he could help out on another part of the project until his main role really needed him again. He confided that in the past he would have laid low and no one would have been any the wiser. He was so impressed with the up-front moves by the project leader to be more tolerant, concerned and open with team members that he felt it was safe to mention his present position.

2. **Having a clear set of responsibilities** that allows people to know where they should be making judgements and where it is not their business.

LEARNING FROM EACH OTHER

The personal gains from working in multi-disciplinary teams far outweigh the frustrations that are also inevitably part of the deal. If your attitude is one of wanting to learn and improve the breadth of your knowledge then you will have more fun from the whole experience as well as being a much more interesting person to work with.

Across traditional functions

Build up a data base of experience, interests, knowledge and abilities of all team members for reference by all. Make this facility known to other teams as well, where there is an interface with what you are doing. Use this information, first in discussion and then in work applications to broaden the way you approach your work.

Through team performance reviews

Do a regular evaluation of how well the team is performing as a team. Give people constructive feedback about their contributions, and be prepared to listen and act upon feedback that you receive in turn. If someone finds you touchy and irritable it is much better that you learn about it and make improvements than to have people avoid you and keep you out of the main stream of activities.

Responsibilities to other teams that come after you

When your project is complete but before the team disbands, put together an outline document of the lessons you have learned in the process of working on the project. Then work out ways in which you can pass on your knowledge to other, newer teams so that they can benefit from your experiences.

What can you learn from earlier teams that came before you in the company?

Talk to people who have led or been involved in earlier projects and ask them what they have learned from their experiences, and particularly from their mistakes. Those of you who have seen any of the *Video Arts* training videos will understand the power of learning from seeing things done the wrong way!

ENCOURAGING THE WIDER PROJECT TEAM

Involving customers

Much has been made in this book about the need to be customer focused, and Chapters 1 and 2 give guidance on specific techniques to achieve this. However, another perspective is to involve customers in the project itself and to make them a genuine part of the team. Some ideas about how customers can be incorporated into the structure of a team are suggested in the next chapter.

In this section we suggest some processes you might adopt to encourage customer involvement.

Research

- Focus groups to identify needs and explore reactions.
- Synectic groups (or creative workshops) to create ideas and explore directions.
- Quantitative research for size and segmentation.
- Stated preference techniques for product definition.
- Hall tests of models.
- Tracking research post launch.

Other

- Development team visiting or working with customers.
- Trade visits to your team.
- Recruiting staff from customers.
- Inviting key customers to join development team.
- 'Partnership developments'—tailored for one customer.
- User groups.
- User database—direct marketing.
- User response cards.

Involving suppliers

Thinking further about the total group of people who will have an influential part to play in your product development, it is often true to say that certain suppliers can be key to its success or failure. If this applies to your project, how can this situation be managed to best effect? There are two models of managing supplier relationships in common use.

The Western model—multiple sourcing

Recent experience in many companies has shown that a number of serious problems with this approach are common:

- antagonistic relationships, trust missing on both sides;
- encourages competition on price not quality;
- encourages short production runs;
- lost learning-curve benefits;
- cost of multiple tooling and set-up.

The Japanese model—partnership sourcing

The alternative approach, based on Japanese practices, is now becoming widespread amongst forward looking Western companies as well. It features:

- tiers of linked vendors;
- sometimes linked by common share-holdings;
- shared long-term planning;
- rapid response and dedicated relationships;
- make or buy decisions made early;
- vendors who can be chosen at the concept stage;
- vendors who can be integrated into project team;
- shared risk;
- encouraging a long-term view of vendor appraisal;
- encouraging the use of quality criteria for selection;
- encouraging open information sharing;
- CAD/CAM links.

AN ATTITUDE OF TOTAL QUALITY

Chapter 2 covered the specific quality issues that relate to product development. In this section we look at the subject from the team's perspective—how to develop a quality *attitude* as the shared state of mind of members of your team.

The current move to 'total quality' rather than 'quality' reflects a shift in emphasis from product quality alone to that plus everything else. This outlook is very much in keeping with integrated product development. After all, customers don't just want the 'product', and the sooner this is taken into account in the development process the better.

- They want it delivered on time.

- They want to be able to operate it intuitively.

- They want to be able to understand manuals.

- They want to be invoiced accurately.

- They want to be treated well if they have to telephone us for information or simple reassurance.

and so on.

The other strong link between NPD and total quality is the emphasis on involving everyone in an organisation (both vertically and horizontally) in meeting customer needs.

An integrated team working in an organisation already committed to total quality has a head start, with team members from widely different disciplines sharing the same attitudes and understanding of this approach. For such teams this section will serve as a reminder of some of the key points that characterise total quality.

Teams attempting integrated product development without an organisational culture committed to total quality will not have the same advantage. This section will give them a very brief introduction to the total quality approach. An important move for such teams will be to try to gain a common understanding and acceptance of this approach from everyone who makes an input to the team's work.

All of those involved in integrated product development will benefit from understanding these basics of total quality. Most importantly, they should become ingrained as a shared attitude towards the standards that are acceptable for anyone and everyone working on the project at every stage. When you don't have tight functional and authoritative control over the work people are doing you do need them to believe in the same quality standards.

The key points from total quality that will help to improve team working in NPD are.

1. The definition of quality for everyone in the team is conformance to customer requirements, demanding constant attention to the relationship between supplier and customer whether internal or external.

2. Prevention is almost always better than correction. Thinking

ahead, putting effort into planning, calculating risk are important procedures that we cover elsewhere, particularly in Chapters 3 and 7. A team working on NPD needs to share this attitude.

3. You are aiming for a standard of *zero defect*. This is attainable, even given variation, as long as you conform to your customer's requirements. Producing wire that is always between 0.95 and 1.05 metres is zero defect if that meets your customer's agreed needs.

4. Your method of working should keep you mindful of the quality wheel: the plan-do-check-action (PDCA) cycle (Figure 5.2). *Plan* relates to the design of services and products and planning to implement them; *do* is the production process, followed by marketing and selling activities; *check* implies checking the process and conducting customer satisfaction surveys; *action* wraps around to the beginning of the cycle again, involving redesign to take account of any customer dissatisfaction. In team work this cycle helps to emphasise the constant interaction between different aspects of the whole development process.

5. Make sure that you all have a clear and constant sense of purpose that drives all your effort.

6. Continually improve your processes; even within the lifetime of a short development project there will be room for improvement in the way you work.

7. Learn on the job. Everyone in the team should want to achieve self-improvement through working on the project.

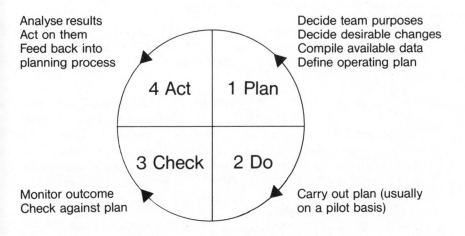

Figure 5.2 The PDCA cycle

8. Encourage leadership not only from the team leader, but in their own areas from other team members as well. (More on leadership in the next section.)

9. Drive out fear so everyone can work effectively for the project and the company.

10. Break down barriers between departments. This is as fundamental to total quality as it is to integrated product development. It happens through continuous effort and by following the other quality rules.

LEADING AND FOLLOWING

This section looks at the different styles of leadership that can be appropriate at different stages of product development.

Styles of leadership

In the next chapter we describe how teams go through different stages as the life cycle of the product development advances. Not surprisingly this demands changes in style from the person leading the team.

One broad distinction of behaviour or style in leadership produces these two categories:

• Autocratic, task orientated, directive. Such leaders define the goals of the team, plan how to achieve them, indicate how each member will contribute and direct the action of the group.

• Democratic, person orientated, showing consideration, participative. These leaders communicate with individual team members, show trust, explain actions and show regard for group members.

These categories may be convenient but there are some conceptual traps. For example, we don't try to fit everyone into the categories 'tall' and 'short' just because these labels anchor two ends of a continuum. So, too, most leaders probably fall somewhere between these categories, not necessarily into one or the other. Another trap is to come to the conclusion that the categories are mutually exclusive—this need not be so. For example, one could be quite directive but still show consideration.

It is therefore worth looking at a broader range of styles. As a project leader you can afford to be quite self-conscious about what you are doing under different circumstances, and the following style descriptions may prove to be a useful shorthand to help you decide how you should act at different times of the project's life cycle.

Directive leading

The directive style of leadership means keeping a tight hold on the reins and maintaining control. This is what's needed when the going is tough and there are hard deadlines looming in the very near future. Adopting this style puts a lot of pressure on the project leader. It is also unlikely to be popular with team members. It is important, therefore for the leader to prepare the team for the possibility that under certain circumstances this is the style he or she will be adopting.

Delegative leading

At the other end of the spectrum is delegative leading, an appropriate style when the team members are highly competent and have clear objectives, and when the whole plan is going like clockwork. When using this style the project leader has little personal involvement and in most cases will be working away on his or her own technical part of the development programme.

Participative leading

A participative style is based firmly on consensus decision making. This style comes into its own at crunch decision points. It should be adopted by the project leader to retain the future commitment of the team members. Participation in decisions that will have repercussions for the team's future actions is the key factor. This kind of involvement obviously slows things down, and is therefore not advisable when there is a real 'mad panic' on. The better planned the whole project is, the more chance there is of applying this style at the right times, to good effect.

Consultative leading

The consultative style means that the leader still makes decisions, but confers with team members to get their views and input on areas where they have the expertise. This style is most appropriate at the very early stages of a development project when the leader is in the process of building up an overall framework and needs to gather a considerable amount of information to do this.

Negotiative leading

The negotiative style is probably the most valuable leadership style of all for the individual running a product development team. The power of persuasion has to replace the power of authority in the day to day running of integrated teams. At best, the negotiative leader will be able to get right inside the skin of extended team members: understand their needs, their feelings and their frustrations. Only then will he or she be able to do deals with them that will have an effect.

Styles of 'followership' amongst team members

What about the other side of the deal? Everyone who has had to lead or manage other people will tell you that one of the biggest variables of all is the particular individual you are trying to manage. If you can understand something of the character of the person you are dealing with in leading a development project you can cut down significantly on misunderstandings and wasted time.

Receptive team members

These are the people who prefer to be given clear instructions and set deadlines. With such directions they can then get on with their bit, happy in the knowledge that they are doing what is required of them.

Reciprocating team members

At the other end of the scale are those individuals who resist and resent direction from above. They respond better to the negotiative, rather than the directive, style of leadership and will drive some hard bargaining before they can be persuaded to do what is asked of them. The reciprocating team member will regularly give the leader a hard time, constantly questioning their authority, and generally making life difficult!

Self-reliant team members

These people prefer to work without constraint and will have lots of their own ideas to contribute to the project, especially if they are allowed just to get on with them as and when they feel they fit in. It is important for the team leader not to swamp the self-reliant type and to learn the difference between showing an interest and interfering. This is where the delegative approach to leadership comes into its own.

Collaborating team members

These people really want to be part of the process and will be amongst the first to offer their services to help, even on peripheral activities. They are great believers in the collaborative decision making process and will need to be sure that they are involved at the stage when the decision is made. They are all in favour of trying out new methods.

Informative team members

These are the people who like to provide ideas and views, but are quite happy for others to make the final decision. True democrats, they will support the final decision even if it does not match their previously held view.

Handy's 'best fit' approach

Charles Handy sees leadership in a way that is particularly valuable for the complexity of the context of product development. He links the leader, team members, the task and the organisation. The first three, themselves all some function of the fourth, are linked by seeking a 'best fit' between them along a continuum
TIGHT...............FLEXIBLE.

- A leader is at the tight end if he or she is directive and towards the flexible end if supportive.

- The team members are at the tight end if they don't like ambiguity and want structure, but are at the flexible end if they are intelligent, competent and self-actualising.

- The task is at the tight end if it is of short duration, routine, or a closed problem, but at the flexible end if it requires creative solutions and is protracted.

In theory, locating these three elements so that they occupy the same relative positions on this continuum should make for a good team. It makes the point yet again that there is no absolute right or wrong where leadership is concerned. It's a case of horses for courses.

PROBLEM SOLVING

Understanding the process of problem solving, and having familiarity with some specific techniques, can be a tremendous help in achieving good results from a wide and varied team.

Problem solving is usually divided into these phases:

1. Select and define the problem
2. Determine the causes

3. Formulate possible solutions
4. Select the most promising of these, and plan
5. Implement the solution
6. Monitor progress and evaluate the outcome.

At this point, depending on your success or lack of it, you may well re-enter the process at stage 1 by refining the problem and continuing through the other phases. This division is not hard and fast, and there will always be grey areas. Nor may the sequence be as linear as the above suggests.

For example, the problem may be that production of your new product is below expectation: the third party company producing it is slow to respond to the additional features you need them to include. That might be because you are slow to pay them. You are slow to pay them because your cash flow is poor. So the real problem is cash flow and how to improve it.

Here we have gone from stage 1 (problem definition—productivity) to stage 2 (causes) back to stage 1 (new problem definition—cash flow).

Expansion and contraction

Having ideas is central to problem solving, so we need to incorporate methods to expand our thinking. Interactive skills are important here too, because we have to create an environment where people feel 'safe' and where they are willing to make their contribution. The section below on communication will cover this subject in more detail.

At a certain stage we need to focus our thinking; to select the significant problem(s) from all of those that have a potential claim on our time. So we need to consider techniques that allow us to eliminate alternatives and to home in on that which is important.

Finally, we have to commit ourselves to 'closed loop' problem solving. This means we don't just assume that because we have attended to a problem and implemented a solution that the thing is actually working. We need to emphasise the need to monitor progress and to take account of changed circumstances. 'Open loop' problem solving is the opposite. It assumes that attending to the problem is what counts, after which you can leave it alone.

CONFLICT RESOLUTION

Conflicts will arise in multi-disciplinary teams. This is a healthy sign, not a sign of failure, but it is important to know how to handle conflict when it arises. The combined effect of the team processes described in this chapter should be to prevent large-scale conflicts at the team level. What this section concentrates on is the inevitable conflicts that arise between individuals who bring different attitudes, values and approaches into the team.

Conflicts arise because of incompatibility. One practical way of dealing with this has been designed by Thomas and Kilmann.* Their Conflict Mode Instrument is designed to assess an individual's behaviour in conflict situations. Armed with this information about yourself and a fellow team member/protagonist, you have the means to work through a conflict rather than allowing it to accumulate and prolong bad feelings.

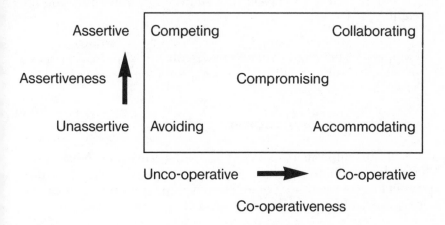

Figure 5.3 Analysis of conflict

The analysis of conflicts shown in figure 5.3 describes behaviour along two dimensions: (1) assertiveness, the extent to which the people attempt to satisfy their own concerns, and (2) co-operativeness, the extent to which people attempt to satisfy the other person's concerns. These two basic dimensions of behaviour are used to define five specific methods of dealing with conflicts:

• Competing
• Accommodating
• Avoiding
• Collaborating
• Compromising.

*Thomas, Kenneth (1975) *The Handbook of Industrial and Organisational Psychology*, Vol II, edited by Marvin Dunnette, Rand McNally, Chicago.

Competing

This style is assertive and uncooperative—people pursue their own concerns at the other person's expense. Competing might mean 'standing up for your rights', defending a position which you believe is correct, or simply trying to win. This style can be useful:

- when quick, decisive action is required, particularly at the crucial closing stages of a development project;

- where an unpopular course of action has to be taken such as cost cutting;

- on issues vital to the project's welfare when you know you are right;

- to protect yourself against people who take advantage of non-competitive behaviour such as in outside negotiations on pricing or specification, or internal negotiations for resources for the project.

Accommodating

This style, the opposite of competing, is unassertive and co-operative. When accommodating, people neglect their own concerns to satisfy the concerns of the other person. In development projects it can be appropriate under the following sorts of circumstances:

- by the team leader, to help team members experiment and learn from their own mistakes;

- when you realise that you are wrong, to allow a better position to be heard, to learn from other people and show that you can be reasonable;

- when continued competition would only harm your cause;

- when preserving harmony and avoiding disruption are especially important.

Avoiding

This style is unassertive and unco-operative—people using it are not pursuing their own concerns or those of the other person. It does not address the conflict, and is seldom the right way to act in teams. Possible applications are:

- when diplomatically side-stepping an issue;

- if postponing an issue until a better time;

- when simply withdrawing from a threatening situation.

Collaborating

This style is both assertive and co-operative—the opposite of avoiding. This is what you are really aiming for in good team work. Collaborating involves an attempt to work with the other person to find some solution which fully satisfies the concerns of *both* persons. It means digging into the issue to identify the underlying concerns of the two individuals and to find a mutually acceptable alternative. Collaborating between two persons might take the form of exploring a disagreement to learn from each other's insights; resolving some condition which would otherwise have individuals competing for resources; or confronting and trying to find a creative solution to an interpersonal problem. Collaborating is the best style when you want:

- to find an integrative solution when both sets of concerns are too important to be compromised;

- to learn through understanding of the views of others and to test your own assumptions;

- to merge insights from people with different perspectives on a problem;

- to gain commitment by including other people's concerns into a consensual decision;

- to work through personal bias which will interfere with a working relationship.

Compromising

This style is intermediate in both assertiveness and co-operativeness. The objective is to find some expedient, mutually acceptable solution which partially satisfies both parties. It falls on a middle ground between competing and accommodating. Compromising gives up more than competing but less than accommodating. Likewise, it addresses issues more directly than avoiding but doesn't explore them in as much depth as collaborating. Compromising might mean splitting the difference, exchanging concessions, or seeking a quick middle-ground position. This style can be useful to achieve temporary settlements to complex issues, or to arrive at workable solutions under time pressure.

Conflicts will arise because of the difficulty of what NPD teams are trying to do, and because by their nature they are made up of people from different disciplines, with different outlooks on life and work.

DECISION MAKING

The complexity of the integrated approach to NPD that we are advocating means that decisions by teams and individuals have to be taken with all seriousness.

The psychology of team decisions

Making decisions involves choosing between alternatives. As a general rule, more information leads to better decisions. There are of course exceptions. But, given the value of information for making decisions, one clear advantage of team compared with individual decisions is the additional information that comes from the involvement of a number of people.

- Teams not only increase the amount of information available but also the number of decision-making strategies, compared with lone workers.

- The processes of communication within a team make for a clarity in understanding the issues around a decision that is difficult to achieve working alone.

- Team members can be encouraged to play devil's advocate during discussions leading to decisions, thereby reducing the chances of ignoring counter-arguments.

Conditions when a decision would be better made by an individual than a group include:

- the need for a quick decision;

- when the problem is relatively simple and straightforward;

- when the decision is not of great importance.

Team decisions can be dangerous!

There is a popular misconception that whereas an individual may make a hasty, rash, and ill-considered decision, a group is likely to be much more temperate and sensible in its recommendations. We now know this simply isn't true, and there is a large number of well documented catastrophes attributable to group decisions that bear this out. In particular, teams should be aware of and on their guard against two group phenomena, *risky shift* and *groupthink*.

Risky shift and group polarisation

Risky shift is a term used to describe the tendency for a group to opt for riskier decisions than would an individual. For example, an NPD team may be told that there is a new technology available that provides some user benefits but is completely unproven in practice. Given the high risk of failure, how does the team decide whether to try the new technology?

Quite consistently, and against original predictions, groups will opt for actions which are riskier than those chosen by individuals. Why? Early explanations favoured:

- diffusion of responsibility;

- risk-taking individuals who dominate and sway the group.

But more recent evidence favours:

- culture: risk taking is valued in our society;

- competition: when recommendations are compared, individuals compete to become at least as risky as the others, or even more so.

- kudos: because risk is valued, arguments in favour of risk seem more persuasive than cautious arguments.

It has also become clear that risky shift is an instance of a more pervasive group characteristic, that of group polarisation. A group is likely to arrive at recommendations more extreme than those favoured by the individual members beforehand. Thus a noise-abatement group will recommend a maximum noise level below that thought reasonable by its individual members earlier on.

Warning: when a group meets to discuss a cherished ideal, value or project, the chances are that the decision it reaches will be extreme! Refer back also to Chapter 3 on risk, especially the checklist.

Groupthink

Groupthink, identified by Harvard psychologist Irving Janis, embodies elements of risky shift and group polarisation, but is even more pathological. A team that falls victim to groupthink will not only be riskier, but will defend itself vigorously against reality testing. Janis maintains that Pearl Harbour, MacArthur's invasion of North Korea, the Bay of Pigs, and the escalation of the Vietnam war are all disasters than can be laid at the door of groupthink. The human and material cost of these is incalculable.

Note: because of the political impact of groupthink, examples are commonly drawn from this arena; however, the principles apply just as much to decisions about the launch of a new product or the penetration of a new market.

These are the characteristics of groupthink:

- An illusion of invulnerability.

- Collective efforts to rationalise, to ignore warnings, and to accept assumptions.

- Total belief in the group's inherent rightness.

- Stereotyped views of the competition as weak and stupid.

- Pressure on any group member who questions the group's assumptions and stereotypes.

- Self-censorship by individual members of doubts and counter arguments.

- An illusion of unanimity (even when this is lacking).

- The evolution of mindguards, individuals who take it upon themselves to 'protect' the group from undesirable information.

Here are some consequences of groupthink drawn from the Bay of Pigs affair (1961):

> *Assumption*:   'No one will know the USA is responsible for the invasion'.
> BUT daily papers in the USA were, at the time, publishing stories about probable action by America against Cuba.
> *Assumption*:   'The Cuban air force is totally ineffective'.
> BUT it was not, and inflicted heavy damage.
> *Assumption*:   'The landings will spur Cubans to revolt against Castro'.
> BUT the CIA already had evidence which showed Castro to be very popular.
> *Assumption*:   'If the invasion force meets opposition it can retreat into the hills'.
> BUT maps of the area showed that an invading force would be trapped.

Avoiding groupthink

Groupthink is not inevitable. After the Bay of Pigs, Kennedy took special steps to prevent its recurrence during the Cuban missile crisis, and this was resolved successfully.

These were the differences:

- No one was regarded as 'the expert'. In NPD you also want to encourage as much cross-fertilisation as possible.

- Everyone was responsible for each issue being discussed. But don't take this too far in NPD. (See the section on responsibility charting in the previous chapter).

- Members were encouraged to challenge statements to see if they were sound. This is very worthwhile advice for multi-disciplinary teams.

- The group did not isolate itself. If you have co-located, pay special attention to this one, and make sure that there are enough openings for you to get to the outside world and for it to get to you. Nor must your special area become out of bounds for other people in the company.

- New people were brought in to challenge existing decisions and make new suggestions. This is good practice and is one of the ways of keeping members of the extended team involved, even when their specific expertise is not being used.

- The leader did not attend all sessions and this reduced conformity needs. Try this.

- Simple stereotypes about the 'Ruskies' (the competition) were avoided and moral issues of right and wrong were discussed. In NPD this would equate to an examination of all issues with respect to the project's objectives, and in particular examining benefits and costs from the customer's point of view.

These general principles for avoiding groupthink remain valid today, and should be debated and learned by all NPD teams!

Striking a balance

Striking a balance is by no means easy. The very forces that lead to groupthink are desirable in moderation. These include a tendency to preserve friendly relationships, consensus seeking, protecting others from disturbing influences, and the pursuit of approval. Just the kind of thing you might see in a happy, healthy work group.

And while it must surely be good to challenge statements and assumptions, an over-critical atmosphere can kill any willingness to contribute new (and hence not very well thought out) ideas. It is estimated that one 'yeah but' objection generates sufficient negative energy to swamp three 'attaboy's!

The answer is for top management to monitor the progress of groups in which they are not over-involved (because for the group leader is just as prone to groupthink as the rest), to know about the symptoms of groupthink, and to be vigilant against it. See the suggestion in Chapter 6 that a company 'heavyweight' (and from time to time other evaluators) be involved from the early stages of the project to help fulfil this function.

Conclusion

Good decisions are based on sound information, the plentiful generation of quality alternatives, and appropriate criteria for selecting them. Teams can help with all these stages, with one clear caution: to avoid the considerable dangers of groupthink.

GOOD COMMUNICATIONS

The guidelines in this section are intended mainly for within-group communication and as such are part of good team processes. In addition there are some important points to be made concerning communications and contact outside the project team:

- Identify and use your resource investigators (see step 3 of team building in the previous chapter).

- Keep close and regular contact with your customer and when possible include a customer as a member of the project team.

- Maintain close contact with department managers of your team members.

- Keep your own manager adequately informed at all stages. An important consequence of this contact is that you will need to earn the right to be protected from outside demands when your project reaches a crucial stage.

The most important aspects of good communication for team working are:

- good listening skills;

- understanding your own weakest areas in communication;

- accepting criticism constructively;

- responding to positive messages;

- knowing how to say no; and

- knowing how to express positive and negative messages.

Good listening skills

Listening is different from 'not talking'. If you are going to communicate effectively in a wide and multi-disciplinary team then one of the first things to learn to be is a good listener. It is surprisingly difficult, and for this reason we often refer to quality listening as 'active listening'. You may not look as if you are doing anything, but

if you are listening actively, you are actually working quite hard.
    There are several characteristics of active listening.

Reflection

From time to time you show your attention by reflecting back to the talker something that she or he has said, such as 'So she was full of unexplained marketing jargon?'

Open questions

These help the talker continue, without which there is not much listening to be done! 'Did you finish on time?' simply calls for a 'Yes' or 'No' answer, but 'Tell me about the highlights of that last part of the project' opens the conversation up.

Don't interrupt

You will chip in from time to time, but choose your moment. Don't cut across your speaker, and definitely resist the temptation to complete his or her sentences. Consider the information content of what the person is saying and think how you can make use of the information they are conveying. How can this tag on to something you already know?

Eye contact

An unblinking stare is a bit daunting, but so is someone who steadfastly refuses to look at you. You must meet the talker's gaze from time to time to show your interest and concern. Arrange the seating so that it feels natural for you, avoiding head-on arrangements.

Appropriate body language

Don't claim to be interested while stifling yawns, or claim to have plenty of time while trying to get an oblique glimpse of your watch. These things are noticed!

Avoid hasty conclusions

This is very important, because what we believe has quite an impact on what we 'hear'. If you reach too early a conclusion, you will have trouble assimilating (in a neutral way) the rest of the speaker's message.

Omission

Think about what the person is *not* saying. This will give you clues about what their particular areas of difficulty are.

Exploring possible problem areas

It is useful to be able to narrow down areas in which you may experience difficulties, as well as identify those where you excel. In Table 5.1, we have listed down the page things that you might do from time to time, such as express positive or negative feelings. Across the page we have the people or groups with whom you interact. The cells lie at the intersections of activities and people.

If you can identify a cell that describes a problem area, put a number in it: 1—if it is a small problem, through to 5—if it looms as a major problem for you.

For example, if you can express negative feelings with most people, but never your department manager then you might put a 3, 4 or 5 in the cell corresponding to the department manager column, second row down.

When you have finished the whole table, add up the numbers in each column, and pencil in the totals underneath the table. Do the

Table 5.1 Identifying communication problems

	Team leader	Team member A	Team member B	Team member C	Department manager	Sales persons	Total
Express positive feelings							
Express negative feelings							
Refuse requests							
Express personal opinions							
Express justified anger							
Accept positive state-ments							
Total							

same for each of the rows in turn. Add the numbers horizontally, and pencil in the total on the right hand side of the table. This simple exercise should help you identify areas worth working on; be they activities or people, they will show up as the larger totals.

Being criticised

We don't know anyone who actually enjoys being criticised, and the object of this discussion is not somehow to make it fun. What we are trying to do is to recognise that criticism (when justified) is a mechanism for keeping us on target when we are deviating. In team working this is a crucial element of good communication.

Because criticism can come as a bit of a shock, we need to look at reactive styles so that we can improve our standards on the one hand without having our self-esteem reduced to tatters on the other.

- **Aggressive**: This style may be the basis for that well-known saying 'the best means of defence is attack'. A person in this mode will flare up, fight back, get personal, and try and deflect the issue. Worst of all, he or she will not be in the right frame of mind to act on the criticism and change their behaviour.

- **Passive**: Passive people have a tendency to assume the worst. 'Yes, you're right, I'm hopeless, I can never perform to standard, and do you perhaps have a vacancy for a doormat?' You can add to this the passive-aggressive style. This person is grievously wounded (and shows it), but 'bravely' bears up under the strain to soldier on; the net effect is to put most critics off for good.

- **Assertive**: As we said earlier, no one enjoys criticism, but we can respond to it positively. The first thing is not to accept all that is said 'uncritically'. *Note*: this is not the same thing as rejecting criticism. For example, you might be criticised for being late—you think you've been on time. Your response might be 'I think you're mistaken; as far as I know my time-keeping is good. Could you tell me why you thought there was a problem?' Of course, you might be late from time to time. Your response should be 'You're right. I have a problem with time-keeping. I'm working on it. If you could let me know of particular difficulties that have resulted, I'll do my best to rectify them.'

Here is a checklist of stratagems for when you have to react to something threatening, such as criticism.

- Don't overreact by being angry or upset. Stay calm.

- There is no need to interpret criticism as a personal attack on you. It is something you are doing that needs correcting. Your self-esteem can survive it.

- Listen carefully. Acknowledge all of it, some of it, or none of it as appropriate. Be honest with yourself and with your critic.

- Ask for explanations of the parts of the criticism that you do not agree with.

- Especially if you disagree with some of the facts, use the technique of 'buying time'. Here, you neither accept nor reject the criticism; you simply suspend your judgement pending further information, and you make this clear to your critic.

Responding to a positive message

People are sometimes surprised that any coaching is needed to help us cope with positive messages. The fact is that the British rather downplay effusiveness and emotionality, so that most of us are ill-equipped to deal with compliments.

As an exercise you might like to think about what the aggressive and passive responses to a compliment would be. Here are a few pointers to appropriate behaviour:

- Reflect on a compliment in much the same way as you should reflect on criticism, with honesty. Is it fully justified? Partly? Not at all? The latter is quite important, because it implies that the person is trying the manipulate you, or to ingratiate.

- It follows that it is wrong to reject a compliment out of hand.

- Don't treat it as a joke either. Someone who is trying to recognise your good points is not going to enjoy having that thrown in his or her face. Your apparent self-deprecation is a rejection of what they were offering you.

- Accept a compliment politely: 'Thank you, I appreciate your saying that.'

- It is probably a sign of good personal development if you can add to the compliment: 'You liked the exhibit? I'm so glad, I thought it worked out well too.'

How to say no

Most of us find that saying 'No' is difficult to do. There are many reasons for this. We are raised to be compliant, and we fear that turning someone down will make them dislike us (the odd thing about this is that we seldom do the same to people who turn us down, so the fear is irrational). Another reason is our own failure to see that we are just turning down a particular request; it is not a rejection of that person in themselves.

When might you need to decline something or someone? First of all, we are not talking about legitimate tasks that might be assigned to you. If you write software and the team leader assigns an area of code to you, then get on with it. What we want to consider here are unreasonable requests, requests which, for the reasons outlined, we often agree to when we shouldn't. This isn't good. We end up feeling resentful, and if we lose control over this tendency to passive acceptance, our 'real' work will suffer.

Good communication is all about respecting rights. Remember, you have rights too, and if you respect them, while at the same time not trampling over someone else's, then you will benefit and so will those who work with you.

When you must react to (what might be) an unreasonable request:

- The first survival tactic is to buy time. This stops you being 'put on the spot'. You just say 'I have a lot on, so I'll need time to think about that. I'll let you know this afternoon'.

- Use 'I' messages rather than waffle on about 'They wouldn't like it if they thought I was helping you.' Try instead 'It's true that I've finished this part of my work, and I can see that you are pressed for time. What I have to do is plan out my next activities which will take a couple of hours, then I'll be delighted to help you out for the rest of the day'.

- One 'I' message to try and avoid is the 'I can't'. It sounds like an excuse and as though you are somehow not responsible for your own actions.

- Express your feelings. You probably feel bad about saying no, so say so. It really does take the sting out of a refusal. 'I can see what this means to you which is why I feel so dreadful about turning you down. After four evenings staying late I promised myself a night at the theatre and I'm looking forward to that. I hope you can find someone to help'.

- You may have to revert to the 'broken record' technique to overcome persistence. 'Yes I know it's urgent, but my time is fully booked. I'm really sorry Meg is ill, but my time is fully booked. Gosh, I didn't realise you had an ulcer through worry, how awful for you, but my time is fully booked.' They'll get the message (in the end).

A final point about rights. It's all a question of balance. If you respect yourself, and your rights, you will be a content, well motivated and capable team member. However, you will also respect the rights of your team, such as its right to expect loyalty, flexibility and effort from its members. What we have been discussing here are techniques to prevent you from becoming ineffective because you are 'the one who won't say no!'. The exploiters can't or won't get organised themselves.

Expressing disagreement

Many of the remarks made in the previous section apply here. We are fearful of being different, controversial, or 'negative' because of the possible withdrawal of approval or affection. It is well worth while overcoming these reservations, both for personal reasons, and for the sake of the team. Uncritical acceptance of another's point of view can result in flawed ideas being put into practice.

- State clearly the fact that you disagree.

- Be constructive. Not 'That just won't work' but rather 'Will that lead to . . .?' or 'The difficulty I foresee is . . .' or 'How about getting around it this way . . .?'

- Distinguish your opinion from fact. 'As I see it . . .'

- Avoid spurious references to hidden authorities to bolster your argument. 'Everyone knows that . . .' or 'It is well established that . . .'

- Be willing to change your opinion in the light of new information. 'In view of what you've just said I can see . . .'

- Recognise the other's point of view. 'I appreciate that it affects you differently . . .' or 'You have put a lot of effort into this, but it may be worth considering . . .'

How to send a positive message

Consider the case where you wish to compliment someone. Here are some guidelines.

Step 1: Prepare yourself—be sure that you mean what you are saying. Don't use praise as a carrot to make people work harder.

Step 2: Maintain good eye contact while you are speaking.

Step 3: Use 'I' messages—take ownership of what you are saying about them.

Step 4: Be precise and specific in your compliments—this comes across as more sincere than generalisations. Thus 'You handled that awkward customer very well' rather than 'Generally speaking, you're good at handling people'.

How to send a negative message

Consider the case where you have to criticise someone. A good exercise in empathy is to remember what it feels like to be criticised. Bear in mind that what you are trying to do is to correct a tendency, not demolish a person.

Step 1: Choose and arrange a suitable time for the discussion.

Step 2: Prepare yourself by writing a script or using role play.

Step 3: Use 'I' messages to express your feelings.

Step 4: Acknowledge any positive aspects of what you are commenting on.

Step 5: Criticise behaviour, not personality.

Step 6: Restrict your comments to specific instances; don't fall into generalisations. Thus avoid 'You're hopeless at managing your time'. Instead try 'You missed the deadline for that report'.

Step 7: Stick to your point, using the broken record technique if necessary.

Step 8: Aim for criticism that is constructive rather than destructive.

We have dwelt on good communication because it is such a difficult thing to get right, yet is so crucial to good team work. At every stage of new product development it is worth while for team members to work to improve the quality of their communication with one another and the wider team they are involved with.

6

Team Structures and Team Development

SETTING THE CONTEXT—THE ORGANISATIONAL STRUCTURE

Few project leaders are in a position to change the organisational structure that they work in—though increasingly people are taking this into account in their personal job moves. Nevertheless it is useful to understand some of the help and constraints on product development and other project work that are associated with different organisational structures.

The functional organisational structure

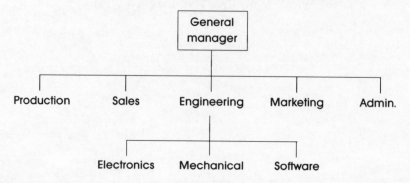

Figure 6.1

This structure is really designed for control, for example over budgets, personnel and technical resources. However, with its emphasis on functional decisions and communications, it does not encourage the vital cross functional approach that integrated product development depends on.

The project organisational structure

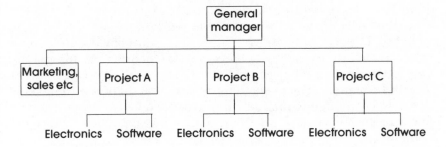

Figure 6.2

This structure allows people to demonstrate their loyalty to the project, with the specific bonus of providing a focal point for external customer relations. The downside of this structure is the problem of where people go once their project is complete, along with minimal opportunities for technical interchange between projects.

The matrix structure

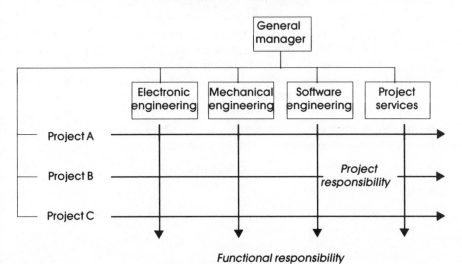

Figure 6.3

Considered for years to be the structural answer to true project management, the matrix structure allows functional groups to exist in their own right. These functional groups exist mainly to resource and support projects. Experience has shown that matrix organisations are costly to run and run into difficulties concerning conflicts of interest. With good team working practices, however, there is a much greater chance that they will work. Refer in particular to the section in the previous chapter on conflict resolution.

A large part of the effort needed to work in a successful matrix goes into understanding the other person's point of view and seeing what they are trying to achieve in the context of the whole organisation. General or resource managers and project managers need to negotiate effectively to make sure that all of the right skills are being exploited to the full. Their work can be greatly assisted by the appropriate structuring of the teams working along the project dimension.

Structuring teams is about drawing together the right resources:

- to do the best quality job

- in the shortest possible time

- within an acceptable budget.

This, then, is the highly complex juggling act that the project leader in new product development has to contend with every day.

How can we structure teams to help rather than hinder? In the first place we can learn an important lesson from nature—*form follows function*. This is just as applicable in the organisation of teams of people as it is in colonies of ants or swarms of bees.

Another principle is to be mindful always of what the team is there to do and organise yourself and the team accordingly. Think back to our first step in team building. It follows from this important connection between form and function that there is no one team structure that will always be right. The best way of looking at team structure is in terms of the link between the output—what you want to get done, and the input—from the people available to do it. The nature of the link will be influenced by a number of different factors:

- the degree to which the tasks in the project can be broken down;

- the size of the project;

- how innovative the project is, as opposed to adapting something already basically developed;

- availability of competent staff;

- the technical complexity of the project;

- the personality and style of the team leader;

- the characteristics of the team members.

The best way to structure a team will therefore vary considerably from one development project to another. The best structure will also vary with the phase of the project.

TEAM STRUCTURES AND PROJECT PHASES

In Chapter 3 we discussed the different phases of the product development life cycle with reference to risk containment. Getting the optimal team structure at each phase of the project also helps reduce the risk of project failure by improving the effectiveness of team working under the differing demands of the phases.

Table 6.1, Team structures at different phases of NPD, summarises the points made in this section.

Structural issues in the pre-development phase

In this phase the team leader could be considered to be the person who comes up with the original idea. In many cases it is quite impossible to identify a single 'inventor' because of the way such ideas come into being. Wherever the first germ of the ideas originates, the 'team' that brings it to life should be as wide and amorphous as possible.

Our best picture of the team might be a series of interlocking circles representing top management (as the main decision makers), marketing people and technical people, all in touch with one another on the one hand, and in touch with the outside world on the other. Top management would have good links with commercial and business developments. Marketing people, at least one of whom is likely to be a member of the senior management group, would have good links with actual or potential customers, and good insight into the market place. Technical people would have good links in their own areas of specialisation through research bodies and journals as well as people contacts.

This is by no means a typical picture of a team, but it does fit when we make the link between people and the output from this phase—an original idea—and a clear definition of the company's view of the development objectives (steps 1 and 2 of the product definition process described in Chapter 1).

Structural issues at the concept definition phase

At this phase the team should be narrowed down considerably, possibly to one representative of each of the disciplines involved. At the very least there should be one person from each of the circles of the pre-development phase, along with the originator of the idea. Given that the output must include technical, marketing and commercial objectives, the interdisciplinary make up of this team is essential.

Just as important is the need to focus on getting something specific out. This is why the numbers need to be kept to a minimum—

Table 6.1 Team structures at different phases of NPD

Stage	Input	Output	Team combination	Team types and mix	Observations
1. Pre-development	Views from wide range of people about state of the competitive environment.	Statement of company's view of development objectives.	Top management, techies and marketing.	A very broad, open concept of team. Help should come from everyone when someone comes up with the germ of an idea.	Ideas get generated as the different contributors permute and combine.
2. Concept definition	Stage 1 output.	Statement of what is to be achieved. Success criteria.	Originator of idea, management heavyweight, customer, marketing rep, technical rep.	Co-ordinator leading the team, resource investigators from marketing and technical plants and specialists.	A small 'egoless' team with very broad representation.
3. Evaluation	Data and opinions about feasibility.	Assessment of feasibility, Commercial judgement.	Still owned and pushed by concept definition team BUT gets expanded in the short term by input from wide range of assessors.	An increase in the number of monitor evaluators.	Team is still led by co-ordinator whose role widens to co-ordinate creative and evaluative input by the expanded team.
4. Specification	Understanding of customer wish list and own technical capabilities.	Translation of desire into specifications. Description of technical limits and capabilities. Reconciliation of the two leading to product.	Essentially the same mix as stage 2 but expanded representation by specialists from marketing, technical, and manufacturing not forgetting customers and suppliers.	Maximum interaction between marketing and techies which generates input for … team leader and management heavyweight who pull together the product spec. They provide … constant feedback for specialist teams and may also require access to implementers and completer-finishers.	Getting more specialised but pulling strongly in the same direction.
5. Design and development	Specifications. Capabilities.	A production plan that meets the specification using existing or attainable resources.	Specialist sub-teams for each element of product development—eg a documentation sub-team, a software sub-team, a production sub-team, a marketing sub-team.	Team workers useful to contribute the social skills to help blend the design and development mix.	Important to invest in a good team leader and set up good team processes to pull all the strands together.
6. Production ramp-up	Production plan.	The product.	Similar to stage 5 but a shift in emphasis towards production.	Team leader more in shaper mode than co-ordinator. Implementers and completer-finishers needed to push 'the last 5%'.	The wider team supports the functional production team and continues the parallel development strategy. Avoid temptations to close down the wider team too early.
7. Launch	Product plus all the preparation (marketing, documentation etc.) done in parallel…	Competitive advantage!	Same team structure but reduced time from all except for	Marketing should solicit creative input from others (eg	

probably four to six people. Each person must have a clear input to make, but must also be open-minded enough to take into account the view point of fellow members. For example, each team member should be asked to express the success criteria in their own terms so that the overall standard is realistic and broad based.

However, the real key to success at this phase is that the team members feel they are all building something together. One team member will need to adopt a team role as well as a functional role to make sure that the output is achieved. This person should be a good co-ordinator, in Belbin's terms (see Chapter 4).

Structural issues at the evaluation phase

The core team is still the group that worked out the concept definition, but at this stage they welcome in a range of evaluators from all of the disciplines that could possibly be involved—another company heavyweight (and not the best friend of the current one on the team!); another 'techie' (technician); another marketing person with a different perspective from the existing one; another customer from a different potential market.

It is obviously important for the evaluators to be uninvolved in earlier phases so that they can be clear and objective in the evaluations they make. However, once this phase is over there is no reason why the most helpful and constructive of the evaluators should not be retained in the longer term team if there is a useful role for them in the future. Think back to the discussion about risky shift and groupthink in the previous chapter.

Structural issues at the specification phase

At this phase the marketing person within the core team extends the team to include additional marketing specialists and customers. Their role is to work out expansively what the market requirement is and build this up into a product specification. Simultaneously, the technical person from the core team extends the team to include additional technical specialists, suppliers and possibly third parties. Their role is to define the technical capabilities and build up a full product specification.

The crucial co-ordinating role lands with the team leader, working closely with the company heavyweight. Not only do they need to pull together the two types of information, but they also need to build bridges and keep communication open throughout this whole phase between marketing and technical people.

Structural issues at the design and development phase

The detail in the design will show how the development work can be broken down. The structure you then want to aim for matches the tasks that have to be done with the special skills, knowledge and experience of team members. If further help is required, long or short term, then those resources will need to be negotiated as the phase goes on.

The role of the team leader at this phase is to drive people forward, encouraging good team processes to pull all the strands together.

The structural implications of production ramp up and launch are also covered in the table.

SO HOW CAN WE ENCOURAGE INTEGRATED TEAMS TO WORK?

The traditional hierarchical organisational chart shows vertical relationships between people, usually based on control, and indicating the expected channels of communication.

If we are to succeed in integrating teams across the company we need to re-configure these channels of communication by seeing the organisation in a new way. In particular we need to develop new, *horizontal* communication channels across the company. This different way of seeing an organisation has become known as *networking*. There are some dramatic consequences when a company is prepared to work as a networking system. Managers need to set the example by communicating well and openly across the company. People working on projects can often be prime movers through their own behaviour, and will reap the benefits.

What are we aiming for in integrating teams? The kinds of changes associated with networking systems include:

- more and better information exchange between people across the company who previously had little or no contact when they were looking at the organisation in hierarchical terms;

- an informal, open atmosphere where you don't have to think 'should I be speaking to this person?' who happens not to be in your division or project team;

- broad involvement in decisions;

- searches for help on projects going beyond the immediate team, and starting to involve outsiders both within and outside the company;

- in time, a possible move away from the one-person, one-boss mentality to more of a sense of shared responsibility to achieve the company mission;

- managers being able to go beyond their functional boundaries and provide support where it is needed;

- a real sense of interdependence and co-operation between project teams working for the greater good of the whole company;

- quality standards are felt to be a team responsibility, with everyone playing their part to maintain and improve those standards.

What practical steps can we take to achieve this kind of company?

It is one thing to have a mental picture of the kind of company that works as a network system with integrated teams: it is another thing to make it happen in your own company. In this section we look at some of the steps that can be taken by managers and project team members to get there. We do want to encourage team members to be proactive and try out some of these methods. Those that are particularly successful may then become adopted by other teams and other parts of the company.

- Ask yourselves if you fully understand the company's vision and mission, to the point where you can see where your department or project fits in to it.

- Build up a database of experience, interests, knowledge and abilities of all team members for reference by all, and make this facility known to other teams, particularly those where there is a known interface.

- Make sure that your project goal and outline project plan are available on a database that is accessible by everyone in the company. Then other people will be able to chip in and share the workload, led by the company's vision and mission, and using the knowledge base to the full.

- You all know about critical success factors in your own jobs—extend this concept within the team to working out the 'critical linkage factors' that exist between your project and all of the other projects that are going on in the company—make it your business to find out what they are.

- Develop a glossary of the terminology used in projects so that everyone involved in any project in the company can be confident of speaking the same language:
  —list the main terms used in projects;
  —think of all the different ways these terms are defined and used;

  —produce a glossary with the best agreed definitions for each
  term.

- Brainstorm with your team to establish what steps you could
  take to make your project more visible to the rest of the company.
- When your project is complete, before the team disbands, put
  together an outline document of the lessons you have learned in
  the process of working on the project. Then work out ways in
  which you can pass on your knowledge to other, newer teams so
  that they can benefit from your experiences.

TEAM DEVELOPMENT

Our final approach to team structures is to take a look at the different
stages they go through over time. For example, in a long project the
core team working through the design and development phase may
go through a number of the phases listed below.

Most analyses of team development end up with a description of
four stages. The value of understanding something about the stages
is the same as parents needing to understand something about
child development—for example to know that the temper tantrums
you are being subjected to are a regular part of the 'terrible twos'
phase. Better to know what the regular patterns are so that you are
prepared, and can take appropriate action.

The terminology used: *Forming, Storming, Norming, Performing*
is a bit clichéd, but not bad to aid memory. You may prefer to think
up your own terms but they should be memorable and reasonably
descriptive.

Stage 1—forming

Note that many teams never get past this stage, to their own and the
company's loss.

Characteristics:

- more a group of individuals than a team;
- people trying to establish where they fit in;
- uneven participation—the extroverts do all the talking;
- no one owns up to their weaknesses;
- not much enthusiasm, though there may be excitement about
  what you are embarked upon;
- no serious decisions get made.

Communication hints:
To help the team move through this stage to stage 2:

* spend time in one to one discussions with other team members so you get to know each other better;

* deal with any small conflicts, don't avoid them hoping they will go away—they will just get bigger in the next stage;

* ask lots of questions of the team leader and other members— even if you are afraid they seem stupid, you can always prefix them with 'this may be a stupid question but . . .'

* listen well to the others so that you get to know their quirks;

* check that you have worked through the five steps of team building given above.

Stage 2—storming

Even a short-term project team should be aiming to get to this stage after a couple of weeks.

Characteristics:

* members are prepared to be more risky and experiment with new ideas;

* real conflicts of values and interests are likely to arise;

* feelings are expressed more readily;

* people are starting to establish processes and procedures, but just as many people are failing to use them, or using them in the wrong way.

Communication hints:
To help the team move through this stage to stage 3:

* review the project goals;

* review repeatedly the ground rules that you are working to;

* make sure you participate fully in meetings, and try to encourage the quieter team members to have a say;

* don't stamp on other people's ideas—rather try to build on them;

* do as much joint problem solving as you can.

Stage 3—norming

You will do very well to get to this stage in a project team and we are probably talking in terms of months into the team's life.

Characteristics:

- obvious focus on the project goal;
- real sense of commitment to the project;
- a greater sense of confidence and trust in one another;
- sound decisions are being made on important matters;
- sense of pride in what has been achieved so far.

Communication hints:
To help the team move through this stage to stage 4:

- organise training sessions so that you can understand more about the disciplines of other team members;
- hold sessions where you make a point of learning from your experiences and mistakes so far;
- increase the amount of contact you have with other parts of the company—other project teams and other functional areas;
- improve on the amount of communication you all have with customers and suppliers.

Stage 4—performing

It will have to be a very long-term project team to reach this stage. More often it is permanent work teams that have the luxury of attaining stage 4.

Characteristics

- definitely an agile, healthy middle age rather than senility;
- emphasis on thinking ahead and on continuous improvement;
- strong sense of trust and ability to accept mistakes from one another;
- fully democratic style of working;
- empowerment allowed by the leader and accepted by team members.

Communication hints:
To help the team continue to work at this stage:

- regular talk in terms of continuous improvement in everything you do;
- ask for more responsibilities;

- take on a mentoring role for teams in the company at earlier stages of development;

- be proactive in seeking contacts with customers and potential customers inside and outside the company.

7

Planning and Controlling Integrated Projects

INTRODUCTION

The need for careful and well managed planning has been stressed many times in this book, not least as a vital part of controlling risk and reducing time to market. We have also seen that it is not only needed to achieve the physical goals of the development, but it is also an integral part of building an effective and productive team.

Although new product development has its own particular problems, planning NPD can be approached in the same way as planning any important project. This is possible because managing NPD shares all of the characteristics that distinguish *project management* from any other branch of management science. These characteristics include:

Goal orientation: A project is a set of activities carried out to achieve a specific goal, and the main objective of project management must be to achieve this goal. In a 'good' project management environment, this should be overwhelmingly the most important activity of the project manager, with as many of the other burdens of management taken on by others or accepted to be of lower priority. Chapters 1 and 2 discuss the techniques needed to translate from company objectives to product development objectives, which become in turn the *goals* of the project.

Finite duration: A project has a finite duration, and as a good rule of thumb, any set of activities that does not (eg product support) is not best managed using entirely these techniques.

Unique: Whilst it is not always true that all projects are unique in *every* sense, if the complete set of goals and activities *are* repeated, then other management techniques may bring a greater degree of control, and otherwise be more effective.

Bring about planned change: This is also more true from the converse; a set of activities designed to maintain the *status quo* is not normally a project, and is probably better managed by other means. Project managers should therefore regard themselves as agents of change and thus be dynamic and motivated to achieve.

Self-contained: In order to bring about a specific goal there is always a self-contained set of activities that will achieve it. It is not always the case that a single project manager can be given responsibility for all of these activities, and several people may therefore contribute towards the project management of that particular goal. The importance of this is that if a project must be managed in this environment, it must be made very clear what the interfaces are between each area of management responsibility. Ideally there should be one person with overall responsibility for the goal, who makes sure that individual project managers can't say 'I thought *he* was doing that'!

Multi-disciplinary: Depending on how the boundaries of the project are defined (see above), this may not always be a characteristic of project management, but it is extremely common. As has been argued earlier in this book, it is vital in product development.

Those contributing in one way or another to the achievement of a product development project would include:

- Marketing
- Customers
- Engineering (software and hardware, development and production)
- Industrial design
- Documentation
- Manufacturing
- Suppliers
- Production control
- Quality control
- Sales
- Service and Support
- Finance
- Human resources
- Administration.

For one reason or another, the large majority of project managers come from a technical or engineering background and tend to be familiar with the language of similar disciplines. However, if they are to be effective in the above environment, they will have to understand the terminology and approach of the other disciplines involved.

One of the roles of the project manager is therefore to act as an interface between a number of different disciplines.

Goal orientation

Arguably the most important aspect of projects is that they set out to achieve a specific goal. This has been discussed in detail in Chapters 1 and 2, but it is worth reiterating the main points.

The company will only be successful if it can develop successful products. However, products do not exist in isolation; a 'good' product is only good when judged in context; ie it must:

- match market needs;

- generate value to customers;

- use technology and design to achieve competitive advantage;

- be developed rapidly;

- not be unnecessarily risky;

- fulfil all legislative and safety requirements;

- be economically viable (including the recovery of development costs!).

Therefore the overriding goal of project management in this context must be launches of product that:

1. Are on time and to budget.
2. Are what the market wants.
3. Satisfy the market's quality requirements.

Project management must be totally committed to achieving this.

Dimensions of the goal

It should be obvious from this that there are three dimensions to the goal:

Time
Expenditure
Achievement

where the latter includes all aspects of the deliverables, including quality and product cost.

Immediate objectives

To translate the above into more immediate and tangible objectives you need to be able to answer three questions:

1. **Who** is the project aiming to satisfy?
   More immediately than 'the market', there will be a person or people within your organisation who will stand in judgement of the project as it progresses and at the end. You need to know who they are, what they expect from the project and whether there are goals that have not been made explicit and may not be in any way embodied in the project deliverables. Make sure that you talk to them directly to uncover these hidden goals.
2. **How** will success be measured?
   Make sure you understand these measures in all of the relevant dimensions. Time and expenditure are relatively easy to quantify and tend to be the first to be fixed (but make sure you know what leeway exists on both). Physical achievement is somewhat harder but *must* be defined to the same degree. Lists of deliverables will form the backbone of this, probably coupled with quality criteria that may either be company wide or specific to the project (see QFD in Chapter 2).
3. **How** will you know you are getting there?
   This is what this chapter on planning and control is all about! This introduces a structure for effective planning and control during project management generally, and new product development specifically.

PLANNING

Project planning is almost always acknowledged to be one of the key responsibilities of project management, yet it is often treated as an exercise just needed to keep senior management happy! Clearly the need for planning goes much further than that, as is explained below.

Why plan?

To highlight objectives

The very act of planning can, if carried out properly, be of great help in clarifying the goals of the product development project. The planning process will translate the original objectives into the detailed physical outputs (the deliverables) in a way that is meaningful to the people who have to achieve them. The process of translating objectives into deliverables is not always as straight-forward as it may seem, and may require considerable input from the project team as well as from those people who are depending on the output of your project. This should always involve referring back to the earlier documents in the development cycle, and in particular to the 'concept specification' (or whatever document defined the original objectives) and to the QFD chart (see Chapter 2).

A key project management task is to ensure that the deliverables from the project are *necessary* and *sufficient* to achieve the true goals of the development. This means that effort should not be spent on things that aren't needed ('creeping excellence' is a good example of this), but on making sure that every detail is attended to when it is needed. The latter is particularly important in the later phases of product development.

To reduce uncertainty

The role of planning in risk reduction and risk management and hence the reduction of uncertainty is fully covered in chapter 3.

To improve efficiency

There are two dimensions to this. The first and most obvious is in the use of elapsed time. The techniques of network analysis used in project planning are purpose made to work out the order in which to carry out tasks in order to finish the project in the minimum time.

The second, and often more important, is to utilise resources within the company in the best possible manner. It has to be admitted that this is more difficult in a multi-project environment with shared resources, and that project management tools are less good at helping the project and resource manager achieve optimum efficiency. However, the more sophisticated software packages contain facilities to help, and these must be used intelligently to improve resource efficiency.

To set realistic expectations

Decisions about whether to proceed with a project must be made on the most realistic estimates possible. In the same way, judgements about the success or failure of the project should be based upon what was actually possible.

Given that there is all too frequently a gap between what was planned and what actually happens, it is necessary to distinguish two components to this. The first is a *real failure*, ie a shortfall between what was possible in the circumstances and the actual outcome. It is this that the project should really be judged on. This is very often exacerbated by *planning failure*, ie a gap between what was actually possible and what was stated to be possible in the plan. In reality the project success will be judged on the sum of these two components.

Good planning can narrow the gap in two ways. The first is that by careful attention to detail it is always possible to reduce the planning failure. There may be a temptation to 'over-plan' ie to allow for more resources or time than you need. This must be avoided because there will often only be a small gap between what makes the development project viable (in terms of cost or time) and what is not viable. If you over-plan, you run the danger of the project being rejected, or of over-committing company resources when they could be better employed elsewhere.

The second way in which planning can help, is that by improving efficiency it should be possible to get much closer to that achievement that is ultimately possible than would otherwise be the case.

As part of the control process

Plans are not independent entities to be produced and then ignored, but are an integral part of project control. They should delineate the exact work content, clarify what needs to be produced, and produce good measures of progress during the project. Progress measures should exist in the three dimensions of a project:

> **Time**
> **Resource usage**
> **Achievement.**

To achieve the full degree of control available, certain conventions and 'rules of thumb' need to be adopted in the planning process that will be detailed later.

To ensure effort is applied at the right time

There is a natural desire to 'get on with it' and to move as rapidly as possible into the implementation or development phase of the project. The pressure to do this comes as much from company management as from keen engineers, but must be resisted.

Chapter 5 showed why a phased approach should be adopted. This should not be treated as an artificial structure but as real and concrete with objectives for each stage. This requires the correct amount of effort to be put into each stage.

There is a rule of thumb that says that an error that might cost £1 to fix at the design phase will cost £10 to fix in production and £100 after being shipped. There is plenty of evidence to suggest that this principle can be extended to the whole product development process (although the actual factor may need revision!). This is confirmed by the observation from recent studies in UK manufacturing companies, that typically 80 per cent of the total product cost is determined during the design phase (Figure 7.1).

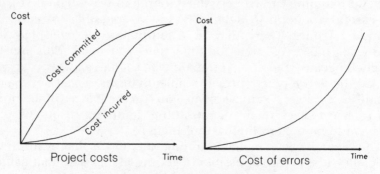

Figure 7.1 **Expenditure differentials**

This goes hand in hand with the general observation that project costs increase dramatically as the process nears completion. Expenditure is normally low during concept development, evaluation and specification, increasing during design and implementation and is often just as high during production and marketing.

However, if the phasing is handled correctly, the converse also applies—the greatest influence on overall project success occurs early in the process and effort has a diminishing effect on the 'goodness' of the outcome as the project proceeds (Figure 7.2). This may be obvious considering the influence of getting the details of the specification correct, but it applies equally to whether you are developing the correct product!

Figure 7.2 **Influence on project success over time**

The upshot of all this is that companies *must* be prepared to put the appropriate amount of effort into the early phases of product development if they are to improve their overall performance. A well structured planning process should encourage this. Chapters 1 and 2 illuminate the details of the early activities required for ultimate success.

Incremental planning

We have already discussed the need for a phased approach to the life cycle of a project and how knowledge and certainty increase during the process. There is an exact parallel with planning—at the outset you will know in some detail what you want to do next, but you will probably only have a hazy idea of the work content of later phases.

Planning should follow this, with a detailed plan of the next phase, or those activities that you can see clearly (a three month horizon might be typical), but only a rough outline of the future beyond that. In this way the 'planning focus' moves forward as knowledge of the next stage increases.

Even though the precise details of later stages may not be known, it is still necessary to plan them in whatever detail is known, in order to estimate time-scales and resource requirements. However, it should be clearly understood what degree of accuracy exists for each phase. To avoid the wrong impression being given, you should not add more detail to these phases than required.

Plan contents

For the avoidance of doubt, a plan is not a bar chart and a bar chart is not a plan! A good and useful project plan will contain most if not all of the following.

Summary—milestones and costs

The complete document is going to be quite long, so make sure you include a summary of everything senior management should remember (in case this is the only bit they have time to read!). It should, as a minimum, include the overall cost of the project and a list of the milestones that you accept responsibility for. A milestone should always be associated with a physical, provable fact, eg a deliverable, a project review, audit acceptance etc. Milestones should not be included for anything whose completion is open to interpretation, as this will only cause problems later.

Taking stock

A statement or discussion of the current position—what is known, what has been done so far, and how this project fits into the big picture. This is often the main subject of another document (eg the acceptance report from the previous stage), but it is still worth including a summary in the current plan, so a complete picture is maintained in one document, showing the exact position when the plan was written. If there is a gap between phases this becomes more important.

Clarify objectives

A simple statement of what you are expecting to achieve by carrying out the plan. Clarify in what way this has evolved from the original objectives set out in earlier documents. Make sure you do not include unnecessary detail (eg by including internal deliverables) that will not directly affect the success or failure of the project.

State assumptions

There will normally be a mass of assumptions behind every plan, so an exhaustive list is not appropriate, just those that are important. The major one is that in stating you will be complete by a certain date, you are assuming that you start by a given date, and that the resources (detailed later) are available as agreed.

Other assumptions may actually be sources of risk as well, so be prepared to cover this aspect later in the document.

Strategy

You should state (in general terms) *how* you are going to achieve your goals. A useful way of looking at this is to say:

> 'The goal of this project is to . . .' (objective)
> 'We will achieve this by . . .' (strategy)

This section is intended to make the approach to the project clear— the mass of detail in the subsequent sections may not achieve this very effectively.

Activities

This section will contain the lists or charts normally thought of as 'the project plan'. This will include lists of *activities* with their *dates* together with *who* will be carrying them out. This may take the form of simple lists, or more often as a Gantt chart with bars representing the timing and duration of each task. The layout of the chart may be made to reflect various structures within the project: they could be organised by phase (eg design-implementation-test . . .), by area of responsibility (see Chapter 4, responsibility charting), by resource grouping (eg hardware, software, documentation . . .), by logical dependency, by criticality etc. The company should establish the norm for this.

Resource allocation

It is good practice to state explicitly what resource allocation is assumed in the compilation of the plan. This should be a separate list of resources and their availabilities. This may be implicit in the task list (if they contain resource details), but it should be made clear both for the people concerned and their managers.

Organisation and accountability

Certain aspects of this may be implicit in the company's structure; eg the scope of the project manager's responsibility may be well defined. Any areas that are not covered by default should be explicitly stated.

This is particularly true for the fine structure of the project. Large product development projects in particular may be broken down or organised into sections (eg electronics, mechanics, software etc.), and certain aspects of project management responsibility may be devolved onto others within these areas. See also the section on responsibility charting in Chapter 4.

Alternatively, other team structures could be adopted which may involve technical leadership, administrative control and commercial management being carried by separate people. However, this example is not recommended as it splits up overall project management responsibility into areas with interfaces that are hard to control. If it has to be done, the areas of responsibility must be carefully and explicity defined.

Risks

This section is *always* required, even if only to state that no material risks have been identified.

Every risk identified should be assessed in terms of its likelihood and impact, and most importantly what action has been taken to reduce or avoid it. Contingencies should be clearly stated. Chapter 3 provides a full approach to this subject.

Controls

This may be well covered by company standards and may not need repeating here. Otherwise a description of what control techniques are going to be used should be given, complete with frequency and staffing. This would normally include a list of planned project meetings together with attendance lists. Risk control measures are covered in Chapter 3 and more details of project control techniques are given later in this chapter.

A planning framework

This provides a nine point procedure for developing a project plan.

1. Define objectives
2. Divide into parts
3. Plan the sequence
4. Allocate resources
5. Estimate durations
6. Calculate overall duration
7. Schedule the tasks
8. Agree the plan
9. Communicate the plan.

Define objectives

The first step is to convert the overall goals into deliverable items that can be defined and listed. Chapter 1 refers to the *total product* and this, together with the starter list of launch activities provided in Chapter 3, provides a good framework for the examination of the ultimate outputs required from the project.

Divide into parts

There are many ways of approaching this, but the common element is to take a *top down* approach. Remember that the aim is to identify work packages and not to divide the actual project into separate, non-integrated parts.

This might start with defining the *phases* of the project (eg design-implementation-test), for example to consider the structure and features of the ultimate deliverable (eg hardware, operating systems, application software, documentation, training). One technique that should be included is to refer back to the risk control activity carried out earlier. This should clearly show some priority activities required to reduce or control risks. Whichever method you start with, consider the project from all angles, because each might shed a slightly different light on the steps required to get there.

For each of the parts identified above, define its inputs and its outputs. Make sure that for every input required there is a matching output. Use this fact to identify missing tasks, and to question the need for a task whose output is not another task's input. Determine whether any of these outputs are sufficiently significant to be used as milestones (eg associated with the elimination or control of some major risk).

This process should suggest finer levels of detail, as the examination of required outputs suggests the exact steps required to deliver them.

Plan the sequence

With your list of tasks from the above, how do you think they will occur in terms of time? Don't leave this to a computer to work out—the network should represent *your* picture of how the project should take place, not the other way around.

A critical part of this is to examine external dependencies, ie anything the project depends on that is not carried out by or directly under the control of the project team. This will include supplier activity, the timing of exhibitions, tooling and component delivery lead times etc.

This process will allow you to understand and define the logical dependencies between the tasks which can then be entered into your project planning software.

Allocate resources

Each task can now be allocated a resource (or list of resources) needed to carry it out. This is not an exercise for the project manager alone! It is crucial that the team who will be carrying out the tasks are involved in the planning, and that proper reference to their immediate managers is made (if appropriate within the company management structure—see chapter 6). Team members must accept responsibility for achieving their individual goals, and this won't happen unless they are involved in the planning and estimating process. This activity is also a natural part of the team building process, and was discussed in detail in Chapter 4.

It is worth examining two different models of overall resource usage and allocation. In the conventional approach to product development, it is common to run many projects in parallel. Figure 7.3 illustrates this in simplified terms.

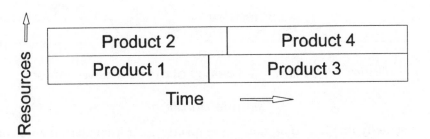

Figure 7.3 Conventional resource usage

During integrated product development, the overriding motivation must be to reduce the time to market. To achieve this, companies need to reduce the number of projects being run in parallel. In the extreme case this would look like Figure 7.4.

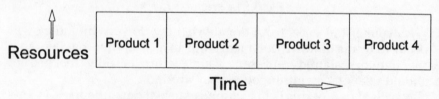

Figure 7.4 Integrated resource usage

This can be a dramatic and sometimes unpalatable change. However, the experience of companies operating in this way is that it *does* achieve significant efficiency increases, as staff are able to concentrate on one project more effectively than on many. It should go without saying that there are limits to how far this can be taken; beyond a certain point the team gets too large (see the earlier discussion on managing interfaces) and the length of the overall project will become limited by other (often external) factors such as tooling lead times and component delivery times. There will therefore be some area of optimum efficiency (Figure 7.5).

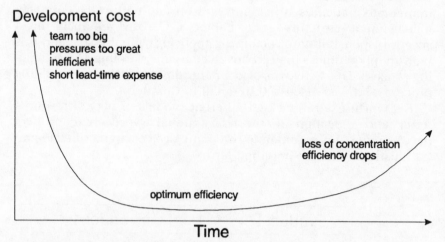

Figure 7.5 Optimum efficiency of product development

Estimate durations

Normally this has to be done in elapsed time rather than man-days due to limitations of some of the software planning tools available.

This limitation is being removed on more recent releases of the more reputable planning packages.

Calculate overall duration

This is done using network analysis techniques by project planning software. The earliest possible end date for the whole project is calculated from the logical dependencies given and the durations of the individual tasks. This process calculates the earliest and latest start and finish dates of each task in the network.

The difference between the early start and the late start of each activity is termed its *float*. Tasks with zero float are critical, and there is always one path of such tasks through the network (and sometimes several). Any delay to any of the tasks on a critical path will delay the whole project.

Schedule the tasks

This is the process by which the dates for each task are calculated according to both the logic *and* the availability of resources to the project. Without this, the plan can be very misleading, as it can lead people to assume a completion date is possible, even though the resources may not be available to achieve it. This is more than just an overall amount of resource for the whole project; if at any stage for any task, more resource is required than available, the project will be delayed beyond its 'early finish date'.

Agree the plan

This will involve negotiating with all of those people affected by the plan. Among them will be those that have to accept the project deliverables, those that provide the resources to carry it out (money and people) and not least, the project team itself.

This may well involve iterations back to any of the earlier steps.

Communicate the plan

Once agreement has been reached, make sure that everyone affected knows what to expect and what is expected of them. Make sure that exact understandings of work content are reached, and test the team's understanding of these.

Some golden rules

These are frequently (but not always) applicable, so use with intelligence!

For project managers:

- **Involve the team in the planning process:** Wherever possible involve the people who will carry out each task when defining it, particularly when estimating durations and resourcing. Responsibility charting described in Chapter 4 provides a suitable means of achieving this.

- **Don't hide fine detail within a task:** If a task you have defined contains resources that come and go in its duration, consider splitting the task down to reflect this. If you don't, even though modern resource scheduling software may be able to cope with this complexity, will you be able to understand what it is doing and why?

- **Don't hide activities between tasks:** If someone is needed to do something affecting your project, give them a task. This is particularly true of delays. If you find you need to insert a delay between two activities, what does this represent? If it represents someone under your control doing something—insert a task. Otherwise (eg it might represent several people outside the project reviewing a document), it might be perfectly legitimate to insert a delay. A task serves to highlight the responsibilities of those involved, a delay is hidden from management control.

- **Make sure that every task has a defined result:** This may seem obvious, but you *must* be sure that you will know when a task has been completed.

- **Choose the lengths of tasks carefully:** There is a balance between all of the above points and the amount of detail in the plan. A good rule of thumb is to keep the length of the majority of tasks roughly the same as the length of the control cycle (how often progress data is collected). In this way very few tasks will be 'in progress' for more than one control cycle, and hence in a state of completion that is difficult to estimate.

  The length of the formal control cycle (see page 177) must be chosen according to the circumstances. In rapidly changing projects (or phases) it might be weekly or even less, provided good information systems exist. It is unlikely to be more than one month. Tasks that are too long can produce a reduced sense of urgency and lower the working efficiency of those engaged on them.

- **Don't create too many tasks:** Considering all of the above, bear in mind that there will be a management burden associated with every task. This occurs in the planning phase when over-complex plans can be a nightmare to set up, and during the control phase when each will need monitoring.

Similar golden rules* for team members would include:

- writing down all your commitments (project and other) and reviewing them frequently;

- making sure your task specifications are written down;

- not releasing your deliverables until they are ready—but allowing others to get on with their next tasks through using informal or early version releases;

- making your own target for completion more aggressive than that you have committed to;

- allowing for time after your task is handed over for tidying-up loose ends;

- allowing time for holidays, sickness and training (15 per cent of the total?);

- being prepared to substantiate your estimates of time-scale—write down how you arrived at them;

- negotiating on task deliverables if the time-scales are impossible to achieve;

- not inflating your time-scale estimates to allow for negotiation;

- being aware of external pressures to deliver early and prepare your reaction to these pressures. Allow for similar pressures on other team members;

- not pressurising others unfairly—reduce the hassle;

- remembering you are a team member—work for the best interests of the project. Accept responsibility for team decisions;

- communicating any bad news early (in writing?);

- being concise and precise in all your communications.

THE CONTROL CYCLE
What is control?

Project control is not just about measuring costs and dates. The following are also part of how a project can be controlled.

- **Giving general guidance and direction:** This is part of the manager's role in translating from the overall objectives into meaningful day-to-day directions. Unless this is considered, projects have a tendency to drift away from their original goals, often producing superb results—but not what was required!

---

*Adapted with permission from Mr W Stoye, Acorn Computers Ltd.

- **Clarifying work content:** Although in an ideal world, every task will have a clearly defined deliverable, in practice there are often areas that need amplification or interpretation. A balance must be struck between the need for explicit task definitions and the time and resource taken to achieve this. In these circumstances the project manager must not just assume that the team know what is required, but must also test this understanding and be prepared to correct it.

- **Ensuring timely flow of decisions and information:** The need for keeping the project team involved with the project is more fully explored elsewhere in this book. However, the manager must keep the team, and others outside the team, informed of what is going on and what has been decided within the team.

- **Setting and monitoring performance standards:** There are many dimensions to this. At its simplest this includes making sure that every team member understands what is required in terms of their performance, ie output, timeliness and quality. However quality may refer both to the output from the task and to the methods used to achieve it. This must be put in the wider context of the company's attitude towards quality, which may mean that the latter is also the responsibility of others in the organisation.

- **Setting reporting and alarm parameters:** In a well-managed system a large amount of data relating to the project is generated. Without care, a great deal of time may be wasted by reporting an unmanageable amount of detail, particularly when it comes to reports sent to more senior management. One task is therefore to determine at what level of deviation from the plan should reports be submitted to others.

- **Taking direct action only when needed:** Although it is very rare for tasks to be completed exactly on time and within budget, not every deviation is going to cause problems. One of the benefits of planning is that it tells you which tasks will have a more serious influence on later deliverables. A good software tool-set will allow you to test the impact of various situations on the overall plan. Management must use a combination of these techniques and their own judgement to determine when to take action.

- **Co-ordinating interfaces:** As discussed earlier, project management is involved a great deal with the interfaces between different people and different disciplines. All of these interfaces must be co-ordinated, feathers smoothed and misunderstandings ironed out.

- **Acting on trends:** The manager must constantly look into the future to make sure that the project is going in the right direction. Small deviations from the original plan may not in themselves ring warning bells, but added together they may spell trouble, either by cumulative effect or by indicating some underlying problem. Not least of these is estimating error, often caused by one person's view—untested against other opinions. Estimating error frequently lies in one direction, normally by underestimating durations.

The control cycle

Collect progress data

Time-sheets are most commonly used for resource usage, and purchase invoices plus expense sheets for other costs. You may also have to set up systems for gathering actual start and actual finish dates for tasks. One of the critical measures is physical progress, which is covered in the next section.

Process the data

Most of this routine progress data is amenable to the use of management information systems for collection and feed-through to project planning tools. This should be done if at all possible to reduce the burden on project managers.

The project plan should be brought up to date to reflect this progress data on a regular basis. This will necessitate repeating most of the actions used to generate the plan (see page 171).

Prepare reports

Bar charts can be used for very simple statements of current *vs.* expected position, on a task by task basis. On complex projects other reports may be used to summarise status (such as earned value techniques).

Analyse status

Where are we now and what does this mean? Project management must use its overview of the project to understand 'the big picture' and avoid getting bogged down in the detail of individual tasks. Planning tools are good at presenting a mass of data in an easy to digest format (eg bar charts), but the manger's task of understanding what this means still remains.

Identify problems

Most importantly the manger must see what is going wrong. This may occur in any of the three dimensions discussed before—Time (tasks or project running late), Resources (overspend) and Achievement (deliverables not being produced or of unacceptable quality or content, product cost turning out too high).

Investigate alternatives

When there are problems, what can be done about them? This should not be an isolated task, because if the team can be involved in solving the problem, they will feel a greater sense of ownership for the remedial action needed.

Communicate

However the solution was arrived at, make sure that everyone affected is informed. There are two areas most often neglected—the customer (or whoever the project is aiming to satisfy) and the permanent record. The latter should be a vital audit trail for the project, recording its history, the decisions taken and why. It is often needed only when it doesn't exist (thus proving Murphy's Law).

Act

Deciding what to do is a waste of time unless you are going to show you care that it gets done. It is surprising how often managers complain that their team doesn't seem to carry out decisions, when the team assume that, as there had been no follow up by the manager, there had been a change of mind!

Measuring achievement

As has been discussed earlier, some areas of progress are easy to measure and for this reason, are often the only aspects measured. This book has stressed the three dimensions of a project and has given plenty of guidance that will help the measurement of the third dimension—physical achievement. There are several techniques which could be used:

- **Subjective:** *'How's it going?'* This will usually elicit a fuzzy response like 'OK'. This is rarely of much use in a control sense, but may be a great help in getting team members to talk about their problems.

- **Pseudo precise:** *'The task is 90 per cent complete'*. This can be of use, provided it is coupled with estimates of remaining duration, and how much effort is required to complete the task.

    Great care must be taken to define and be consistent in the use of percentages. One way of doing this is to extend the idea of 'earned value' by comparing the total cost to date (£s, man days or whatever) with the current (new) estimate of the total cost (on the same basis) at completion. Alternatively, it could be based on 'the percentage of the deliverable performed' in those cases where a suitable measure exists.

- **Precise:** *'Is the task complete—yes or no?'* Arguably the only times you know the real status of a task are before you start and when you have finished—everything in between is guess-work. This is why tasks must have well-defined objectives, and the frequency of the control cycle should match the length of most tasks.

    The answer to the above question should not just be left as yes or no; you should ask for proof that the task is complete and that the output has been accepted by whoever required it as an input. This may require checks for conformity to quality standards as well as completeness of the deliverables.

Key points

For controls to be effective they must be:

- **Appropriately precise:** There is no point measuring the status of your project with any greater precision than is needed, but erring on the side of simple measurements can often hide real problems, particularly cumulative errors.

- **Pertinent:** Measure and control only those aspects (eg the three dimensions) which actually matter to your project. Make sure you are actually measuring what you think you are.

- **Fast:** Status information that arrives late is often completely useless. If you need effective control, eg weekly, aim to set up information systems to report on current status within one day.

- **Consistent:** Use the same measures throughout—both between tasks and during the life of the project.

- **Easy to apply:** Most project managers are overburdened with work, so make sure that whatever controls you use do not add to this unnecessarily.

8

Summary

ADOPT A MARKET FOCUS

We have discussed a seven stage plan for defining products that achieve company objectives and deliver customer delight:

1. **Know what you need to achieve:** Clear, rational thinking is required during the corporate direction setting process in order that it can contribute to better products.
2. **Understand your markets:** This is fundamental to good product development. The process must be outward looking and *must* gather information seen from the customer's viewpoint, not yours.
3. **Define what produces quality:** Customer satisfaction is the minimum goal for any new product development; customer delight is more uplifting and achievable using the technique of QFD.
4. **Develop the options:** Use the company's differential strengths and capabilities to produce different solutions, product elements or configurations that build on the QFD information.
5. **Determine the value of the product elements:** Use conjoint techniques to understand which options generate value in the customer's eyes.
6. **Optimise the value and cost equation:** Trade-offs between total product cost and product features must be made on the basis of real information, not gut instinct. Feature/benefit optimisation offers the tools to achieve this.
7. **Develop the product:** Build the right team and empower them to deliver a well defined goal.

ACTIVELY MANAGE RISK

Risk in NPD must not be accepted passively, but must be investigated and managed actively by the whole team.

- Understand the structure of risk, where it comes from and generally what can be done to reduce it.

- Brainstorm the risks applicable to *your* product using a multi-disciplinary team.

- Decide which risks must be managed based on their likelihood and potential impact.

- Decide how each will be managed or controlled.

- Allocate responsibilities for specific risks to those in the team best able to monitor them.

- Keep risk management a high profile activity throughout the project.

BUILD THE TEAM

In summary, what can the management team do to make sure that the project and task teams in the company are working for the benefit of the overall good? Here is a checklist that may help.

- **Goal orientation:** any team has to work to a clear goal, and the successful integration of teams is highly dependent on a clear, overriding purpose that holds individual team goals together.

- **Accountability:** one person has to take on responsibility for the success of the overall project, and each individual involved in the core and wider team needs to understand what their role and responsibilities are.

- **Respect:** integration will only happen if project team members and leaders behave in a way that respects every individual who has a part to play—within the core team, across disciplines and functions.

- **Break down walls:** create new, informal connections within and outside the company with people who have any input to your project.

- **Involvement:** everyone with an interest in the project should be involved at the earliest possible stage.

- **Planning:** spend time on front end activities—strategies, planning—because of the importance of getting these right in the overall scheme of product development.

- **Cross-functional integration:** make it your business to understand the pattern of relations across departments and functions and to work in a flexible way with people from different walks of working life.

- **Interdisciplinary teams:** the earlier these are formed, the faster and better development works.

- **Heavyweight teams:** get company heavyweights involved in your team—ideally senior managers or board members, from the earliest stage possible.

- **Attention to detail:** slice up the process of work on your project into finite detail so that you can build in corrective action before too much damage is done in any aspect of the work.

- **Empowerment:** avoid short-term power based relationships in the way you go about your work, and take on as much responsibility as you can to contribute to the overall goal.

- **Constructive failure:** make sure it is possible for people in your teams to make mistakes based on an understanding that failure is a crucial part of learning.

- **Wider team:** snuggle up to your customers and suppliers!

- **Persuasion:** the way forward in business is for people to be influential and persuasive in areas where they do not have direct control or authority.

INNOVATE INCREMENTALLY

Large-scale developments are slow and risky. Develop a product range and technical strategy that allows development to take place in smaller chunks.

- Lay down a medium- and long-term strategy that encompasses new technology, new product platforms, product enhancements and planned product replacement or withdrawal.

- Phase the introduction of new technology and features to fit with the above strategy without loading any one development with too much that is new.

- Remember customers want the benefits, not the technology that provides them in itself. Where possible, test new technologies out in existing products through incremental improvements.

- Be prepared to launch new products rapidly and frequently in response to changes in the market.

- Be systematic about how you define each product, and be prepared to do this fast through continuous appraisal of customer information and technological capability.

IMPROVE TIME TO MARKET

The following checklist is given as a summary of many aspects of rapid, customer-focused product development given elsewhere in this book. Apply them not only to current activities, but also to future tasks. Make sure that the plan reflects the resulting view on how all the tasks will be carried out.

Clear task definition

- Am I currently carrying out one task or several? If several, am I still able to work efficiently on each one? Are the relative priorities of each task well enough defined?

- Is what I need to achieve in each task clearly defined? Do I know who will use my output and when they need it?

- How far in the future will I achieve my current objectives? Are they too far away to allow me (or others) to measure real progress? Is it worth considering setting intermediate objectives to aid this?

- How is my deliverable specified? Is the amount of detail restrictive—could the specification be loosened and replaced with more informal agreements between team members?

- Apart from current task(s), is the area of the overall project I am responsible for well defined? Are the interfaces between my area and others clear and well managed? Am I familiar with who else needs to be kept informed of what is going on in my area (remember responsibility charting)?

Overlap inputs and outputs

- What is the bare minimum of information or material I need to be able to start a task?

- When is the earliest this could be available from those providing it? Have I asked them directly? Do they know when I need it?

- Can I do anything to make this information unnecessary?

- Could I use (or make a start with) an earlier version of the materials or information I need?

- Can I learn enough from a 'trial run' (working with the wrong but available information or materials) to make significant time savings when the actual product is ready?

- Can I make assumptions to enable me to work without the information?

- If the assumptions are wrong, how much time will it take to re-do the work?

- What are the other consequences of working to wrong assumptions?

- What other tasks (including other people's tasks) could be started with the information already available to me?

- What information have I produced which would allow others to make some progress?

- What are the risks that such information may turn out to be wrong later?

Don't re-invent the wheel

- Has a similar task been performed before within the company? Can I learn anything (or save some time) by talking to those who carried it out or by studying their outputs?

- Has a similar deliverable (eg product or part of it) been created before, either within the company or elsewhere? Have I studied this to learn what can be applied to this situation?

- Is there a different way of working (and maybe a different structure of deliverable) which allows me to finish the task based on existing information, but that allows very rapid updating when the final information becomes available?

- How will my work be reviewed, verified or tested? Can this be integrated into the duration of the task by way of informal reviews to minimise the review/verification/test time at the end?

Encourage open communication

- What problems do I have now which are slowing me down or preventing me from starting a task?

- Do I feel happy and well motivated about my tasks?

- What worries or uncertainties do I have about my tasks?

- Have I spoken to my team colleagues about these worries?

- Who else might be able to offer advice or solutions?
- How much communicating am I doing in writing? Can I do more verbally?

Glossary of Terms

Burst Nodes

In a logic drawing of the plan, a point at which many tasks depend on one task. These tasks are almost always on the critical path, but can be 'super critical' and should be controlled with great care. They often reflect a project review or the movement of a project from one phase into another.

Core team

People likely to be working full time on a project and probably co-located.

Critical Path

The chain or chains though the network of tasks on which any delay will cause a delay in the project end date. This path is characterised by having zero float.

Deliverable

The output from some activity. It will normally be tangible and must have a recipient (a deliverable must not be created unless someone wants it!). It can be regarded as complete when it is accepted by its recipient (fit for purpose).

Extended team

The other people on whom the success of the project relies, who contribute part-time from inside or outside the company.

Float

The difference between the earliest date and the latest date on which a task can start. In a non-resource constrained world, any task can be delayed within its float without causing an overall project delay. Once a task uses some of its float, subsequent tasks may have their float reduced.

Free Float

Normally used to indicate how long after the (resource) scheduled date a task could be delayed before it causes a delay to the project end date. This does not normally exist in reality as there may be many other resource constraints to take into account.

Gantt Chart   A bar chart of activities where the position and length of each bar indicates the planned timing and duration of the task.

Hammocks   Tasks with no intrinsic duration whose start and end dates depend entirely on other logical relationships. They can be used to allow for management tasks (project management over the whole project duration) and to allow reporting on project phases (by stringing hammocks across the start and end point of each phase and producing reports containing only hammock activities).

Market   A market is a group of customers who are homogenous in some important aspect of their behaviour.

Matrix structure   An organisational structure that consists of functional groups and project groups where any individual is likely to have a 'home' in the former and work in the latter as required.

Milestones   Tasks with zero duration used for reporting purposes to indicate an event of note, such as a dependency on outside events, the end of a phase, or the output of a deliverable.

Moderator   The person who runs focus groups, taking participants through a structured discussion and recording their reactions.

Negative Float   If target dates are used unwisely, it may be that time analysis calculates that the latest start date of a task is before its earliest start date. This cannot occur in reality, so plans should not be left in this state.

PERT   (Programme Evaluation and Review Technique)—uses estimates of most likely, minimum and maximum task durations to calculate overall project duration. In its simplest form it uses the beta distribution to calculate a single duration for each task that is used in network analysis in the normal way. For very advanced applications, Monte Carlo simulation can be used to effectively solve the network for a very large number of combinations of these three duration estimates. This will produce statistical distributions of the project end date and cost that can be used in risk analysis.

Project

A project is a unique set of activities intended to bring about planned change.

Psychometric questionnaire

Psychometrics means, literally, mental measurement. Reputable tests are designed and published by psychologists and should be administered and interpreted by them as well.

Resource Critical Tasks

Because of resource constraints, any delay to these will delay the project.

Responsibility chart

A technique to show who is taking responsibility for which activities in the course of a project, along with information about how the fabric of the team is made up.

Role negotiation

The working out of an agreement between pairs of people to achieve a better working relationship.

Segmentation

Markets are sometimes sub-divided into smaller groups, often based on demographic or lifestyle criteria. Demographic criteria are age, sex, occupation and location. Lifestyle classifies consumers by attitudes and behaviour. In industrial markets, these may be replaced with standard industrial classifications and size criteria.

Team development

The phases that a working team progresses through, partly as a function of time, partly as a consequence of team building actions.

Team building

The actions that allow a working group to achieve the quality of integrated work that can genuinely be described as team work. There are five crucial steps involved in team building, described in Chapter 4.

Team work

This is the state you are aiming for when you want a range of different people to contribute to a common goal. It is characterised by co-operative effort and co-ordinated by clear leadership.

Time now

The earliest date on which any non-started and unconstrained task can start.

Index